Ninja Woodfire Outdoor Grill & Smoker

Cookbook for Beginners

1500 Days of Easy & Delicious Recipes for Ninja Woodfire Electric Pellet for BBQ, Grilling, Baking, Roasting, Dehydrating & Broiling

KAIDA EMBERWOOD

©Copyright 2024 - All rights reserved.

This document and its content are protected by copyright law and international treaties. Unauthorized reproduction, distribution, or modification of this document, which in whole or in part, without the express written consent of the copyright owner, is strictly prohibited.

LEGAL NOTICE:
All rights reserved. No part of this publication may be reproduced, distributed, or transmitted in any form or by any means, including photocopying, recording, or other electronic or mechanical methods, without the prior written permission of the publisher, except in the case of brief quotations embodied in critical reviews and certain other noncommercial uses permitted by copyright law.

DISCLAIMER:
The recipes in this cookbook are intended to inspire and provide culinary ideas. However, the author and publisher make no guarantees regarding the accuracy, suitability, or outcome of the recipes. Cooking techniques, ingredient availability, and individual preferences may vary, and it is the reader's responsibility to adapt and modify the recipes accordingly. The author and publisher are not liable for any errors, omissions, or substitutions made in the preparation of the recipes.

It is important to consult with a qualified healthcare professional or registered dietitian for personalized guidance regarding specific dietary concerns or medical conditions.

CONTENTS

Introduction

CHAPTER 1

GETTING STARTED WITH YOUR NINJA GRILL 1

Essential Tools and Equipment for Woodfire Outdoor Grilling 3

Safety Tips for Outdoor Grilling 1

Grilling Techniques and Tips for Perfect Results 7

CHAPTER 2

FLAVORS, MARINADES, RUBS AND SAUCES FOR WOODFIRE GRILLING 9

CHAPTER 3

DELICIOUS WOODFIRE OUTDOOR GRILL & SMOKER RECIPES 2

Quick Appetizers & Small Chops 2

Grilled Bacon-Wrapped Jalapeno Poppers 2

Smoked BBQ Meatballs 14

Grilled Caprese Skewers 15

Smoked Buffalo Chicken Wings 16

Grilled Bruschetta 18

Smoked Stuffed Mushrooms 19

Grilled Shrimp Skewers 20

Smoked Stuffed Bell Peppers 21

Grilled Halloumi Skewers 23

Smoked Deviled Eggs 24

CHAPTER 4

HEARTY MAIN GRILLED COURSE DELIGHTS RECIPES 26

Smoked BBQ Ribs 26

Smoked Brisket 27

Smoked Pulled Pork 29

Grilled Lemon Herb Chicken 30

Cedar Plank Salmon 31

Grilled Ribeye Steak 33

Smoked Whole Chicken 34

Grilled Shrimp Skewers 35

Smoked Pork Ribs 36

Grilled Salmon with Lemon-Dill Sauce 38

Grilled Vegetable Skewers 41

Smoked Beef Brisket 42

Grilled Portobello Mushroom Burgers 43

Grilled Salmon with Lemon Dill Sauce 44

CHAPTER 5

VIBRANT GRILLED SIDE DISHES AND SALAD 46

Grilled Corn on the Cob 46

Grilled Asparagus 47

Grilled Vegetable Salad 48

Smoked Macaroni and Cheese 49

Grilled Watermelon Salad 51

Smoked Potato Salad 52

Grilled Caesar Salad 53

Smoked Baked Beans 55

Grilled Vegetable Skewers 56

Grilled Caprese Salad Skewers 57

CHAPTER 6

SMOKY GRILLED SEAFOOD OPTIONS 59

Grilled Shrimp Tacos with Lime Slaw 59

Smoked Salmon with Dill Sauce 62

Grilled Teriyaki Tuna Steaks 63

Grilled Lemon Garlic Shrimp Skewers 64

Grilled Garlic Butter Lobster Tails 66

Cedar Plank Grilled Salmon 67

Grilled Cajun Shrimp Tacos 68

Grilled Teriyaki Glazed Salmon Skewers 70

Grilled Garlic Herb Shrimp Skewers 71

Grilled Sesame Ginger Tuna Steaks 73

Smoked Maple Glazed Cedar Plank Salmon 74

Grilled Coconut Lime Shrimp Skewers 76

Grilled Cajun Blackened Red Snapper 78

CHAPTER 7

CREATIVE GRILLED PIZZA & FLATBREAD 79

Grilled Veggie Flatbread with Pesto 79

BBQ Pulled Pork Pizza 82

Grilled Mediterranean Flatbread 83

Thai Chicken Pizza 84

Caprese Grilled Pizza 86

BBQ Chicken Flatbread 87

Margherita Pizza with Grilled Peaches 89

Smoky Sausage & Mushroom Pizza 93

CHAPTER 8

YUMMY SMOKER BURGER & SANDWICH RECIPES 94

Smoky Bacon Cheddar Burger 94

Grilled Portobello Mushroom Burger 96

BBQ Pulled Pork Sandwich 97

Grilled Chicken Caprese Sandwich 99

Spicy Black Bean Burger 101

Teriyaki Pineapple Chicken Sandwich 102

BBQ Brisket Sandwich 104

Grilled Veggie Panini 105

Caprese Grilled Cheese Sandwich 108

Turkey Avocado Club Sandwich 109

Greek Gyro Wrap 110

CHAPTER 9

FLAVORFUL GRILLED BEEF, PORK, & CHICKEN 119

Grilled Beef Burgers 119

Grilled Pork Chops with Maple Glaze 120

Grilled Chicken Skewers with Lemon Herb Marinade 122

Grilled Beef Kabobs with Vegetables 123

Grilled Pork Tenderloin with Mustard Glaze 125

Grilled Chicken Caesar Salad 126

Grilled Pork Ribs with BBQ Sauce 128

Grilled Chicken Fajitas 129

Grilled Pork Tenderloin with Herb Rub 131

CHAPTER 10

DELICIOUS GRILLED VEGETARIAN DELIGHTS 132

Grilled Vegetable Skewers 132

Grilled Portobello Mushroom Burgers 134

Smoked Stuffed Bell Peppers 136

Grilled Halloumi Skewers 137

Smoked Stuffed Portobello Mushrooms 139

BBQ Tofu Skewers 140

Grilled Veggie Quesadillas 141

Smoked Stuffed Zucchini Boats 142

Conclusion 145

Acknowledgement 146

Introduction

Welcome to Woodfire Outdoor Grilling!

Grilling outdoors over a woodfire is a time-honored tradition that brings people together, creating not just delicious meals but also lasting memories. And with the Ninja woodfire outdoor grill, you have the perfect tool to embark on your grilling adventures.

Grilling over a woodfire imparts a distinct smoky flavor to your food, elevating the taste and creating a sensory experience that's truly unmatched. Throughout this cookbook, we'll explore into essential grilling techniques, from preparing and seasoning the grill grates to mastering the perfect sear on your steaks. You'll learn how to grill a variety of meats, seafood, vegetables, and even desserts, impressing your family and friends with your newfound culinary prowess.

This cookbook is designed specifically for beginners who are eager to explore the world of woodfire grilling with their Ninja grill. Whether you're a seasoned cook looking to expand your culinary skills or a complete novice stepping into the realm of outdoor cooking for the first time, this book will serve as your comprehensive guide.

Within these pages, you'll find a collection of delicious grilled recipes that cater to different tastes and dietary preferences. From appetizers and main courses to sides and desserts, each recipe has been carefully crafted to showcase the versatility and flavor of woodfire grilling. Feel free to experiment and make these recipes your own, adjusting ingredients and techniques to suit your personal preferences.

Get ready to experience the magic of woodfire outdoor grilling with the Ninja grill and let this cookbook be your trusted companion every step of the way. Let's ignite the flames, unleash your creativity, and create unforgettable grilled masterpieces that will have everyone coming back for more. Happy grilling!

Chapter 1

Getting Started with Your Ninja Grill

Congratulations on your new Ninja woodfire outdoor grill! Before you dive into the world of woodfire grilling, it's important to familiarize yourself with your grill and gather the essential tools and equipment you'll need. In this section, we'll guide you through the initial steps of getting started.

☑ Unboxing and Assembly:

Begin by carefully unboxing your Ninja grill and ensuring that all the parts and accessories are included. Follow the manufacturer's instructions to assemble the grill, paying close attention to safety precautions. Make sure all the components are securely attached and in proper working order before proceeding.

☑ Read the Manual:

Take the time to read the user manual provided by Ninja. The manual will provide you with specific information about your grill model, its features, and any particular instructions or guidelines you need to follow for safe and efficient operation. Understanding your grill's unique functions and settings will help you make the most of your grilling experience.

☑ Location and Setup:

Choose an appropriate location for your grill that is well-ventilated and away from flammable materials. Ensure that the grill is placed on a stable, level surface, such as a patio or a concrete pad. Avoid using your grill indoors or in enclosed spaces, as this can lead to a build-up of harmful gases.

☑ Fuel Selection:

Wood and charcoal are the primary fuels used for woodfire grilling. Select high-quality hardwood charcoal or lump charcoal, as they burn cleaner and provide better flavor. Experiment with different types of wood chips or chunks, such as mesquite, hickory, or fruitwoods, to infuse your food with unique smoky flavors. Follow the manufacturer's recommendations for the type and quantity of fuel to use with your Ninja grill.

☑ Preheating:

Before you start grilling, preheat your Ninja grill to the desired temperature. The preheating process ensures that the grill grates are hot and ready for cooking. Refer to your grill's manual for specific preheating instructions, as different models may have varying preheating times and temperature settings.

Essential Tools and Equipment for Woodfire Outdoor Grilling

To embark on your woodfire outdoor grilling journey with your Ninja grill, it's important to have the right tools and equipment at your disposal. These essential items will not only make your grilling experience more enjoyable but also contribute to safe and efficient cooking. Here are some must-have tools and equipment for woodfire grilling:

1. **Grill Brush**: A good-quality grill brush is essential for keeping your grill grates clean and free from residue. Opt for a brush with sturdy bristles that can effectively remove food particles and grease build-up.

2. **Long-Handled Tongs**: Long-handled tongs allow you to handle food on the grill with ease and precision. Look for tongs that have a firm grip and are heat-resistant to protect your hands from the heat of the grill.

3. **Spatula**: A sturdy spatula with a broad, flat surface is ideal for flipping burgers, fish, and delicate food items on the grill. Ensure that the spatula has a long handle to keep your hands away from the heat.

4. **Meat Thermometer**: A reliable meat thermometer is a crucial tool for grilling meats to the desired level of doneness. This ensures that your food is cooked safely and avoids overcooking or undercooking. Choose a digital thermometer that provides accurate readings.

- **Heat-Resistant Gloves**: Heat-resistant gloves are a must-have for grilling, as they protect your hands and forearms from burns. Look for gloves made from materials such as silicone or Kevlar that can withstand high temperatures.

- **Basting Brush**: A basting brush is handy for applying marinades, sauces, and glazes to your food while it's grilling. Silicone brushes are heat-resistant and easy to clean.

- **Grill Basket**: A grill basket allows you to cook smaller or delicate food items that may fall through the grill grates. It's perfect for grilling vegetables, shrimp, fish fillets, and more. Look for a basket with a non-stick coating for easy food release.

- **Skewers**: Skewers are useful for grilling kebabs, skewered vegetables, and other skewer-friendly foods. Choose skewers made from stainless steel or bamboo, and ensure they are long enough to keep your hands away from the heat.

- **Chimney Starter**: A chimney starter is a convenient tool for lighting charcoal quickly and evenly. It helps eliminate the need for lighter fluid and ensures a clean-burning fire.

- **Grill Cover**: A grill cover is essential for protecting your Ninja grill from the elements when it's not in use. It helps prevent rust, extends the life of your grill, and keeps it clean between uses.

These are just some of the essential tools and equipment you'll need to enhance your woodfire grilling experience with your Ninja grill. As you gain more experience and explore different grilling techniques, you may find additional tools that suit your specific needs and preferences. Remember to prioritize safety while handling hot surfaces and open flames, and always follow the manufacturer's instructions for your grill and equipment. Happy grilling!

Safety Tips for Outdoor Grilling

Outdoor grilling is a delightful way to enjoy delicious meals and create lasting memories with family and friends. However, it's important to prioritize safety to ensure a pleasant and secure grilling experience. Here are some essential safety tips to keep in mind when using your Ninja woodfire outdoor grill:

Location and Environment

- Choose a well-ventilated outdoor location for your grill, away from any flammable materials, such as overhanging branches, dry leaves, or wooden structures.
- Ensure that the grill is placed on a stable, level surface to prevent tipping or accidental movement during cooking.

Keep a Safe Distance

- Maintain a safe distance between your grill and any combustible items, including outdoor furniture, propane tanks, and buildings. A minimum distance of 10 feet is recommended.
- Keep children and pets at a safe distance from the grill to prevent accidents and burns. Establish a designated safe zone around the grill and make sure everyone is aware of it.

Proper Lighting

- Follow the manufacturer's instructions for lighting your Ninja grill using the recommended methods.
- If using a charcoal grill, avoid using lighter fluid once the coals are already lit to prevent flare-ups. Opt for a chimney starter or other safe lighting alternatives.

Supervision

- Never leave your grill unattended while it's in use. Accidents can happen quickly, and attentive supervision is key to preventing mishaps.
- Stay focused on the grilling process, especially when dealing with high heat and open flames.

Proper Clothing and Protection

- Wear appropriate clothing while grilling. Avoid loose-fitting garments or clothing with long, flowing sleeves that can catch fire.

- Use heat-resistant gloves or mitts when handling hot grill grates, utensils, or hot food.

Fire Safety

- Have a fire extinguisher or a bucket of sand nearby in case of emergencies. Familiarize yourself with their usage before you start grilling.

- In the event of a grease fire, avoid using water to extinguish it, as it can cause the fire to spread. Instead, close the lid of the grill and turn off the burners to cut off the oxygen supply to the fire.

Properly Extinguish the Fire

- After you finish grilling, allow the coals to cool completely before disposing of them in a metal container designated for ash disposal. Never dispose of hot coals in a combustible container or near flammable materials.

- If using a gas grill, ensure that the gas supply is turned off completely after use.

Food Safety

- Practice proper food handling and hygiene to prevent foodborne illnesses. Wash your hands thoroughly before and after handling raw meat or poultry. Use separate utensils and cutting boards for raw and cooked food to avoid cross-contamination.

- Ensure that meat and poultry are cooked to the appropriate internal temperature by using a meat thermometer. Refer to safe cooking temperature guidelines for different types of meat.

By following these safety tips, you can create a secure environment for outdoor grilling and enjoy the pleasures of cooking with your Ninja grill. Remember, safety should always be a top priority to ensure a positive and memorable grilling experience. Happy and safe grilling!

Grilling Techniques and Tips for Perfect Results

Now that you have a solid understanding of the basics of woodfire outdoor grilling, it's time to explore the various techniques and methods that will elevate your skills and help you create delicious meals on your Ninja woodfire grill. In this chapter, we will dive into the art of grilling, covering essential techniques, cooking methods, and tips to ensure optimal results.

Direct Grilling

Direct grilling is a straightforward method where food is cooked directly over the heat source. It's ideal for smaller, thinner cuts of meat, such as steaks, burgers, hot dogs, and vegetables. The direct heat sears the exterior of the food, creating a caramelized crust while retaining its natural juices.

Indirect Grilling

Indirect grilling involves cooking food adjacent to the heat source rather than directly over it. This method is suitable for larger cuts of meat, such as whole chickens, roasts, and ribs, which require longer cooking times. By positioning the food away from the direct heat, it cooks more slowly and evenly, resulting in tender, juicy meats.

Smoking

Smoking is a technique that infuses food with rich smoky flavors. It involves cooking food over low, indirect heat generated by smoldering wood chips or chunks. The smoke envelops the food, imparting a distinct taste and aroma. Smoking is perfect for meats, poultry, fish, and even vegetables, allowing you to experiment with different wood flavors to create unique dishes.

Searing

Searing is a technique used to achieve a flavorful crust on the surface of food, typically meats. By applying high heat directly to the food, you create a caramelized exterior, sealing in the natural juices. Searing is often done at the beginning or end of the grilling process to enhance the visual appeal and taste of the dish.

Basting and Saucing

Basting involves applying marinades, sauces, or oils to the food while it's grilling. This technique adds moisture, enhances flavors, and helps prevent drying out. Use a basting brush to apply the basting mixture evenly, taking care to avoid excessive flare-ups caused by dripping fats or oils.

Rotisserie Grilling

If your Ninja grill is equipped with a rotisserie attachment, you can explore the rotisserie grilling technique. This method involves skewering food, such as whole chickens, roasts, or large cuts of meat, and rotating it slowly over the heat source. Rotisserie grilling ensures even cooking and produces succulent, evenly browned results.

Reverse Searing

Reverse searing is a technique that involves cooking thicker cuts of meat at a low temperature first, followed by a quick sear over high heat. This method allows for precise control of the internal temperature, resulting in a perfectly cooked interior with a flavorful crust on the outside.

Grilling Vegetables and Fruits

Grilling isn't limited to meats alone. Vegetables and fruits can also be transformed into delicious grilled dishes. Grilling adds a smoky, charred flavor and enhances the natural sweetness of fruits and the earthy flavors of vegetables. Experiment with different vegetables like peppers, zucchini, corn, and fruits like pineapple or peaches to create vibrant, grilled side dishes and desserts.

Chapter 2

Flavors, Marinades, Rubs and Sauces for Woodfire Grilling

Enhancing your grilled dishes with delicious seasonings can take your culinary creations to new heights. In this chapter, we will explore various flavor profiles, marinades, and rubs that will elevate the taste of your woodfire-grilled meals on your Ninja grill.

Flavor Profiles

Classic BBQ: The classic BBQ flavor profile is characterized by a balance of smoky, sweet, tangy, and savory elements. It often includes ingredients like brown sugar, paprika, garlic powder, onion powder, cayenne pepper, and a combination of tomato-based sauces and vinegar.

Mediterranean: Mediterranean flavors are vibrant and refreshing. Utilize ingredients such as olive oil, lemon juice, garlic, oregano, thyme, rosemary, and a touch of tanginess from citrus fruits or yogurt-based marinades. These flavors pair well with grilled seafood, chicken, and vegetables.

Asian-Inspired: Asian-inspired flavors offer a blend of sweet, salty, and umami notes. Incorporate ingredients like soy sauce, ginger, garlic, honey, sesame oil, and chili flakes to create marinades and rubs for grilled meats, tofu, and vegetables.

Mexican: Mexican-inspired flavors bring a zesty and spicy kick to grilled dishes. Use ingredients such as lime juice, cilantro, cumin, chili powder, chipotle peppers, and Mexican hot sauces to infuse your grilled meats, poultry, and vegetables with the vibrant tastes of Mexico.

Herb-Infused: Fresh herbs add brightness and depth to grilled dishes. Experiment with rosemary, thyme, basil, parsley, dill, or a combination of herbs to create herb-infused marinades and rubs for various meats, seafood, and vegetables.

Marinades

Marinades are flavorful liquid mixtures that tenderize and infuse meat, poultry, and vegetables with delicious flavors. Here are a few marinade ideas to consider:

Citrus and Herb Marinade: Combine citrus juices (such as lemon, lime, or orange) with olive oil, minced garlic, fresh herbs (like rosemary or thyme), salt, and pepper. This marinade works well with chicken, fish, and vegetables.

Teriyaki Marinade: Mix soy sauce, mirin, brown sugar, ginger, garlic, and sesame oil for a sweet and savory teriyaki marinade. It complements beef, chicken, and tofu.

Yogurt-based Marinade: Combine plain yogurt with spices like cumin, coriander, turmeric, and paprika, along with minced garlic and lemon juice. This marinade adds tenderness and a tangy flavor to chicken, lamb, or vegetables.

Balsamic Glaze Marinade: Create a glaze using balsamic vinegar, honey, Dijon mustard, minced garlic, and a pinch of dried herbs. This marinade works well with pork, beef, and grilled vegetables.

Rubs

Rubs are dry mixtures of herbs, spices, and other seasonings that are applied directly to the surface of the food before grilling. They add intense flavors and create a delicious crust. Here are a few rub ideas:

Smoky BBQ Rub: Combine brown sugar, paprika, chili powder, garlic powder, onion powder, cayenne pepper, salt, and black pepper for a smoky BBQ rub that works well with ribs, pork shoulder, and beef brisket.

Moroccan Spice Rub: Mix together cumin, coriander, cinnamon, ginger, paprika, cayenne pepper, salt, and black pepper to create a fragrant Moroccan spice rub. It pairs beautifully with lamb, chicken, and grilled vegetables.

Herb and Garlic Rub: Blend dried herbs like thyme, rosemary, oregano, garlic powder, onion powder, salt, and black pepper for a versatile herb and garlic rub. It complements a wide range of meats, poultry, and vegetables.

Cajun Spice Rub: Create a spicy Cajun rub by combining paprika, cayenne pepper, garlic powder, onion powder, dried thyme, dried oregano, salt, and black pepper. It adds a bold kick to chicken, shrimp, and grilled corn.

Sauces

Sauces are the finishing touch that adds a burst of flavor and moisture to grilled dishes. Here are a few types of sauces:

Barbecue Sauce: A tangy and sweet sauce made with ketchup, brown sugar, vinegar, Worcestershire sauce, and spices, ideal for ribs, chicken, or pulled pork.

Chimichurri Sauce: A vibrant and herbaceous sauce made with parsley, cilantro, garlic, red wine vinegar, olive oil, and red pepper flakes, perfect for grilled steak or vegetables.

Lemon Garlic Butter Sauce: A rich and buttery sauce made with melted butter, minced garlic, lemon juice, and fresh herbs like parsley or thyme, great for grilled seafood.

Tzatziki Sauce: A refreshing sauce made with Greek yogurt, cucumber, garlic, lemon juice, and dill, perfect as a dip for grilled chicken, lamb, or vegetables.

Flavors, marinades, rubs and sauces are essential elements in the art of woodfire grilling. By exploring different flavor profiles and experimenting with marinades and rubs, you can elevate the taste of your grilled dishes on your Ninja grill. From classic BBQ flavors to Mediterranean, Asian-inspired, Mexican, and herb-infused profiles, there are endless possibilities to explore. Whether you choose to marinate your meats and vegetables or apply flavorful rubs, you'll be able to create mouthwatering dishes that will impress your family and friends.

Chapter 3

Delicious Woodfire Outdoor Grill & Smoker Recipes

Quick Appetizers & Small Chops

Grilled Bacon-Wrapped Jalapeno Poppers

Grill Time: 25 minutes

Serving Size: 6 poppers

Ingredients:

- 12 jalapeno peppers
- 6 ounces cream cheese, softened

- 1 cup shredded cheddar cheese
- 12 slices bacon, halved
- Toothpicks

Instructions:

1. Preheat your grill or smoker to medium heat.
2. Cut the jalapeno peppers in half lengthwise and remove the seeds and membranes.
3. In a bowl, mix the cream cheese and cheddar cheese until well combined.
4. Fill each jalapeno half with the cheese mixture.
5. Wrap each jalapeno half with a slice of bacon and secure with a toothpick.
6. Place the bacon-wrapped jalapeno poppers on the grill or smoker and cook for about 20-25 minutes, or until the bacon is crispy, turning occasionally.
7. Remove from the grill, let them cool slightly, and serve.

Nutrition Information (per serving):

Calories: 210kcal | Fat: 17g | Protein: 9g | Carbohydrates: 4g | Fiber: 2g | Sugar: 2g | Sodium: 390mg

Cooking Tips:

- Soak the toothpicks in water for about 15 minutes before using to prevent them from burning on the grill.

Smoked BBQ Meatballs

Grill Time: 1 hour 30 minutes

Serving Size: 12 meatballs

Ingredients:

- 1 pound ground beef
- ½ cup breadcrumbs
- ¼ cup milk
- ¼ cup finely chopped onion
- 1 clove garlic, minced
- ¼ cup barbecue sauce
- 1 tbsp. Worcestershire sauce
- 1 tsp. smoked paprika
- ½ tsp. salt
- ½ tsp. black pepper

Instructions:

1. Preheat your smoker to 225°F (110°C).

2. In a bowl, combine the ground beef, breadcrumbs, milk, onion, garlic, barbecue sauce, Worcestershire sauce, smoked paprika, salt, and black pepper. Mix well.

3. Shape the mixture into 12 meatballs.

4. Place the meatballs on a smoker rack and smoke for about 1 hour 30 minutes, or until they reach an internal temperature of 160°F (71°C).

5. During the last 15 minutes of cooking, brush the meatballs with additional barbecue sauce.

6. Remove from the smoker, let them cool slightly, and serve.

Nutrition Information (per serving):

Calories: 135kcal | Fat: 7g | Protein: 10g | Carbohydrates: 7g | Fiber: 2g | Sugar: 3g | Sodium: 287mg

Grilled Caprese Skewers

Grill Time: 10 minutes

Serving Size: 6 skewers

Ingredients:

- 18 cherry tomatoes
- 18 small fresh mozzarella balls
- 18 fresh basil leaves
- Balsamic glaze, for drizzling
- Salt and pepper, to taste
- Wooden skewers, soaked in water

Instructions:

1. Preheat your grill to medium-high heat.

2. Thread a cherry tomato, a mozzarella ball, and a basil leaf onto each skewer, repeating until you have 6 skewers.

3. Season the skewers with salt and pepper.

4. Place the skewers on the preheated grill and cook for about 2-3 minutes per side, or until the tomatoes are slightly softened and the mozzarella is slightly melted.

5. Remove from the grill, drizzle with balsamic glaze, and serve.

Nutrition Information (per serving):

Calories: 75kcal | Fat: 5g | Protein: 4g | Carbohydrates: 3g | Fiber: 0g | Sugar: 2g | Sodium: 80mg

Cooking Tips:

- Soaking the wooden skewers in water prevents them from burning on the grill.

- Use fresh, ripe cherry tomatoes and quality mozzarella for the best flavor.

Smoked Buffalo Chicken Wings

Grill Time: 1 hour 30 minutes

Serving Size: 6 servings

Ingredients:

- 2 pounds chicken wings
- 2 tbsp. olive oil
- 2 tsp. smoked paprika
- 1 tsp. garlic powder
- 1 tsp. onion powder
- 1 tsp. salt
- ½ tsp. black pepper
- ½ cup buffalo sauce
- Blue cheese or ranch dressing, for serving
- Celery sticks, for serving

Instructions:

1. Preheat your smoker to 225°F (110°C).
2. In a large bowl, toss the chicken wings with olive oil, smoked paprika, garlic powder, onion powder, salt, and black pepper until well coated.
3. Place the seasoned wings on a smoker rack and smoke for about 1 hour 30 minutes, or until the internal temperature reaches 165°F (74°C).
4. During the last 15 minutes of cooking, brush the wings with buffalo sauce.
5. Remove from the smoker, let them cool slightly, and serve with blue cheese or ranch dressing and celery sticks.

Nutrition Information per Serving:

Calories: 270kcal | Fat: 18g | Protein: 22g | Carbohydrates: 2g | Fiber: 0g | Sugar: 2g | Sodium: 960mg

Cooking Tips:

- If you prefer crispy wings, you can transfer them to a hot grill after smoking to crisp up the skin.
- Adjust the amount of buffalo sauce to your desired level of spiciness.

Grilled Bruschetta

Grill Time: 10 minutes

Serving Size: 4 servings

Ingredients:

- 4 slices Italian bread or baguette
- 2 tbsp. olive oil
- 2 cloves garlic, peeled and halved
- 4 medium tomatoes, diced
- ¼ cup fresh basil, chopped
- 1 tbsp. balsamic vinegar
- Salt and pepper, to taste

Instructions:

1. Preheat your grill to medium-high heat.
2. Brush both sides of the bread slices with olive oil.
3. Rub the cut sides of the garlic cloves on one side of each bread slice.
4. Place the bread slices on the preheated grill and cook for about 2-3 minutes per side, or until lightly toasted.
5. In a bowl, combine the diced tomatoes, fresh basil, balsamic vinegar, salt, and pepper.
6. Spoon the tomato mixture onto the toasted side of each bread slice.
7. Remove from the grill, let them cool slightly, and serve.

Nutrition Information per Serving:

Calories: 163kcal | Fat: 8g | Protein: 4g | Carbohydrates: 18g | Fiber: 2g | Sugar: 3g | Sodium: 197mg

Cooking Tips:

- Use ripe tomatoes for the best flavor.

- Experiment with different bread varieties and toppings, such as mozzarella or goat cheese, for additional variations.

Smoked Stuffed Mushrooms

Grill Time: 45 minutes

Serving Size: 6 servings

Ingredients:

- 12 large mushrooms
- 8 ounces cream cheese, softened
- ¼ cup grated Parmesan cheese
- 2 cloves garlic, minced
- 2 tbsp. chopped fresh parsley
- ½ tsp. dried thyme
- Salt and pepper, to taste ¼

Instructions:

1. Preheat your smoker to 225°F (110°C).
2. Remove the stems from the mushrooms and set aside.
3. In a bowl, mix the cream cheese, grated Parmesan cheese, minced garlic, chopped parsley, dried thyme, salt, and pepper until well combined.

4. Fill each mushroom cap with the cream cheese mixture and place it on a smoker rack.

5. Chop the reserved mushroom stems and sprinkle them over the stuffed mushrooms.

6. Smoke the mushrooms for about 45 minutes, or until the cream cheese is slightly browned and the mushrooms are tender.

7. Remove from the smoker, let them cool slightly, and serve.

Nutrition Information per Serving:

Calories: 120kcal | Fat: 10g | Protein: 6g | Carbohydrates: 3g | Fiber: 2g | Sugar: 2g | Sodium: 220mg

Cooking Tips:

- Choose large mushrooms with sturdy caps to hold the stuffing.

- You can add cooked bacon bits or shredded cheese to the cream cheese mixture for extra flavor.

Grilled Shrimp Skewers

Grill Time: 6 minutes

Serving Size: 4 skewers

Ingredients:

- 1 pound large shrimp, peeled and deveined

- 2 tbsp. olive oil

- 2 cloves garlic, minced

- 1 tsp. paprika

- ½ tsp. cayenne pepper (optional)

- ½ tsp. salt

- ½ tsp. black pepper
- 2 tbsp. fresh lemon juice
- Wooden skewers, soaked in water

Instructions:

1. Preheat your grill to medium-high heat.
2. In a bowl, combine the olive oil, minced garlic, paprika, cayenne pepper (optional), salt, black pepper, and lemon juice.
3. Add the shrimp to the bowl and toss until well coated.
4. Thread the shrimp onto the soaked wooden skewers.
5. Place the skewers on the preheated grill and cook for about 2-3 minutes per side, or until the shrimp are pink and opaque.
6. Remove from the grill, let them cool slightly, and serve.

Nutrition Information per Serving:

Calories: 150kcal | Fat: 7g | Protein: 20g | Carbohydrates: 2g | Fiber: 0g | Sugar: 0g | Sodium: 390mg

Cooking Tips:

- Use large, peeled, and deveined shrimp for easier skewering and faster cooking.
- Soaking the wooden skewers in water prevents them from burning on the grill.

Smoked Stuffed Bell Peppers

Grill Time: 1 hour 30 minutes

Serving Size: 4 peppers

Ingredients:

- 4 bell peppers (any color)
- 1 cup cooked quinoa
- 1 cup cooked black beans
- 1 cup corn kernels
- ½ cup diced tomatoes
- ½ cup shredded cheddar cheese
- 2 tbsp. chopped fresh cilantro
- 1 tsp. chili powder
- ½ tsp. cumin
- ½ tsp. garlic powder
- Salt and pepper, to taste

Instructions:

1. Preheat your smoker to 225°F (110°C).
2. Cut the tops off the bell peppers and remove the seeds and membranes.
3. In a bowl, combine the cooked quinoa, black beans, corn kernels, diced tomatoes, shredded cheddar cheese, chopped cilantro, chili powder, cumin, garlic powder, salt, and pepper.
4. Stuff each bell pepper with the quinoa mixture.
5. Place the stuffed bell peppers on a smoker rack and smoke for about 1 hour 30 minutes, or until the peppers are tender and the filling is heated through.
6. Remove from the smoker, let them cool slightly, and serve.

Nutrition Information per Serving:

Calories: 250kcal | Fat: 6g | Protein: 12g | Carbohydrates: 42g | Fiber: 10g | Sugar: 8g | Sodium: 350mg

Cooking Tips:

- Feel free to customize the filling with your favorite ingredients such as cooked ground meat or different types of cheese.

- You can also top the stuffed peppers with additional cheese during the last 10 minutes of smoking for a cheesy crust.

Grilled Halloumi Skewers

Grill Time: 8 minutes

Serving Size: 4 skewers

Ingredients:

- 8 ounces halloumi cheese, cut into cubes
- 1 tbsp. olive oil
- 1 tbsp. fresh lemon juice
- 1 tsp. dried oregano
- Wooden skewers, soaked in water

Instructions:

1. Preheat your grill to medium-high heat.

2. In a bowl, combine the olive oil, lemon juice, and dried oregano.

3. Add the halloumi cheese cubes to the bowl and toss until well coated.

4. Thread the cheese cubes onto the soaked wooden skewers.

5. Place the skewers on the preheated grill and cook for about 2-3 minutes per side, or until the cheese is golden brown and slightly softened.

6. Remove from the grill, let them cool slightly, and serve.

Nutrition Information per Serving:

Calories: 220kcal | Fat: 19g | Protein: 12g | Carbohydrates: 2g | Fiber: 0g | Sugar: 2g | Sodium: 600mg

Cooking Tips:

- Halloumi cheese is firm and holds its shape well on the grill. Make sure to cut it into cubes that are suitable for skewering.

- You can serve the grilled halloumi skewers with a side of tzatziki sauce or a squeeze of fresh lemon juice.

Smoked Deviled Eggs

Grill Time: 1 hour 30 minutes

Serving Size: 6 servings

Ingredients:

- 6 large eggs
- ¼ cup mayonnaise
- 1 tbsp. Dijon mustard
- 1 tbsp. finely chopped fresh parsley
- 1 tsp. apple cider vinegar

- ½ tsp. smoked paprika
- Salt and pepper, to taste

Optional toppings: chopped chives, crumbled bacon, smoked paprika

Instructions:

1. Preheat your smoker to 225°F (110°C).
2. Place the eggs directly on the smoker grate and smoke for about 1 hour 30 minutes.
3. Remove the eggs from the smoker and let them cool completely.
4. Once cooled, peel the eggs and cut them in half lengthwise.
5. Carefully remove the yolks and transfer them to a bowl. Set the egg white halves aside.
6. Mash the egg yolks with a fork until crumbly.
7. Add the mayonnaise, Dijon mustard, finely chopped parsley, apple cider vinegar, smoked paprika, salt, and pepper to the bowl with the egg yolks. Stir until well combined and creamy.
8. Spoon the yolk mixture into the reserved egg white halves, dividing it evenly.
9. Optional: Top each deviled egg with chopped chives, crumbled bacon, or a sprinkle of smoked paprika.
10. Refrigerate the deviled eggs for at least 1 hour before serving to allow the flavors to meld.

Nutrition Information per Serving:

Calories: 120kcal | Fat: 10g | Protein: 6g | Carbohydrates: 2g | Fiber: 0g | Sugar: 0g | Sodium: 170mg

Cooking Tips:

- For a bolder smoky flavor, you can add a small amount of smoked salt or smoked paprika to the yolk mixture.

- Feel free to adjust the seasonings and add other ingredients such as finely chopped pickles, hot sauce, or herbs to suit your taste preferences.

Chapter 4

Hearty Main Grilled Course Delights Recipes

Smoked BBQ Ribs

Grill Time: 4-6 hours

Serving Size: 4 servings

Ingredients:

- 2 racks of baby back ribs
- ¼ cup brown sugar
- 2 tbsp. paprika
- 1 tbsp. chili powder
- 1 tbsp. garlic powder
- 1 tbsp. onion powder
- 1 tsp. cayenne pepper (optional)
- Salt and pepper, to taste
- BBQ sauce, for brushing

Instructions:

1. Preheat your Ninja woodfire outdoor grill and smoker to 225°F (110°C).

2. In a small bowl, combine the brown sugar, paprika, chili powder, garlic powder, onion powder, cayenne pepper (if using), salt, and pepper to make a dry rub.

3. Rub the dry rub mixture all over the racks of ribs, covering them evenly.

4. Place the ribs on the smoker rack and smoke for 4-6 hours, or until the meat is tender and pulls away from the bones.

5. During the last 30 minutes of cooking, brush the ribs with your favorite BBQ sauce.

6. Remove the ribs from the smoker, let them rest for a few minutes, and then cut them into individual servings.

7. Serve with additional BBQ sauce on the side.

Nutrition Information per Serving:

Calories: 400kcal | Fat: 27g | Protein: 30g | Carbohydrates: 10g | Fiber: 2g | Sugar: 8g | Sodium: 350mg

Cooking Tips:

- For extra tenderness, you can wrap the ribs in aluminum foil halfway through cooking and continue smoking until done.

- Adjust the amount of cayenne pepper in the dry rub to control the level of spiciness.

Smoked Brisket

Grill Time: 10-12 hours

Serving Size: 8 servings

Ingredients:

- 1 (8-10 pound) beef brisket, trimmed
- ¼ cup brown sugar

- 2 tbsp. paprika
- 2 tbsp. kosher salt
- 1 tbsp. black pepper
- 1 tbsp. garlic powder
- 1 tbsp. onion powder
- 1 tbsp. chili powder
- 1 tsp. cayenne pepper (optional)

Instructions:

1. Preheat your Ninja woodfire outdoor grill and smoker to 225°F (110°C).
2. In a bowl, combine the brown sugar, paprika, kosher salt, black pepper, garlic powder, onion powder, chili powder, and cayenne pepper (if using) to make a dry rub.
3. Rub the dry rub mixture all over the brisket, covering it evenly.
4. Place the brisket on the smoker rack, fat side up, and smoke for 10-12 hours, or until the internal temperature reaches 195-205°F (90-96°C) and the meat is tender.
5. Remove the brisket from the smoker, wrap it tightly in aluminum foil, and let it rest for at least 1 hour before slicing.
6. Slice the brisket against the grain and serve.

Nutrition Information per Serving:

Calories: 450kcal | Fat: 30g | Protein: 40g | Carbohydrates: 2g | Fiber: 0g | Sugar: 2g | Sodium: 900mg

Cooking Tips:

- It's important to trim the excess fat from the brisket before smoking to prevent it from becoming overly greasy.

- Use a meat thermometer to ensure the brisket reaches the desired internal temperature for optimal tenderness.

Smoked Pulled Pork

Serving Size: 8 servings

Grill Time: 12-14 hours

Ingredients:

- 1 (8-10 pound) pork shoulder (pork butt)
- ¼ cup brown sugar
- 2 tbsp. paprika
- 2 tbsp. kosher salt
- 1 tbsp. black pepper
- 1 tbsp. garlic powder
- 1 tbsp. onion powder
- 1 tbsp. chili powder
- 1 tsp. cayenne pepper (optional)

Instructions:

1. Preheat your Ninja woodfire outdoor grill and smoker to 225°F (110°C).
2. In a bowl, combine the brown sugar, paprika, kosher salt, black pepper, garlic powder, onion powder, chili powder, and cayenne pepper (if using) to make a dry rub.
3. Rub the dry rub mixture all over the pork shoulder, covering it evenly.
4. Place the pork shoulder on the smoker rack and smoke for 12-14 hours, or until the internal temperature reaches 195-205°F (90-96°C) and the meat is tender enough to be easily shredded.
5. Remove the pork shoulder from the smoker and let it rest for about 30 minutes.
6. Shred the pork using two forks or your hands.
7. Serve the pulled pork on buns with your favorite BBQ sauce and coleslaw.

Nutrition Information per Serving:

Calories: 300kcal | Fat: 15g | Protein: 35g | Carbohydrates: 3g | Fiber: 0g | Sugar: 2g | Sodium: 900mg

Cooking Tips:

- For a smokier flavor, you can use wood chunks or chips like hickory, apple, or cherry during the smoking process.

- Wrapping the pork shoulder in aluminum foil during the last few hours of smoking can help accelerate the cooking process and enhance tenderness.

Grilled Lemon Herb Chicken

Grill Time: 25-30 minutes

Serving Size: 4 servings

Ingredients:

- 4 bone-in, skin-on chicken breasts

- 2 lemons, juiced and zested

- 2 tbsp. olive oil

- 2 cloves garlic, minced

- 1 tbsp. chopped fresh thyme

- 1 tbsp. chopped fresh rosemary

- Salt and pepper, to taste

Instructions:

1. Preheat your Ninja woodfire outdoor grill and smoker to medium-high heat.

2. In a bowl, combine the lemon juice, lemon zest, olive oil, minced garlic, chopped thyme, chopped rosemary, salt, and pepper to make a marinade.

3. Place the chicken breasts in a resealable plastic bag and pour the marinade over them. Seal the bag and refrigerate for at least 1 hour, or overnight for better flavor.

4. Remove the chicken from the marinade and discard the excess marinade.

5. Grill the chicken breasts on the preheated grill for 6-8 minutes per side, or until the internal temperature reaches 165°F (74°C) and the juices run clear.

6. Remove from the grill, let the chicken rest for a few minutes, and then serve.

Nutrition Information per Serving:

Calories: 350kcal | Fat: 20g | Protein: 35g | Carbohydrates: 4g | Fiber: 2g | Sugar: 2g | Sodium: 200mg

Cooking Tips:

- To prevent sticking, oil the grill grates or brush the chicken breasts with oil before grilling.

- For a smokier flavor, you can add wood chips or chunks to the grill.

Cedar Plank Salmon

Grill Time: 15-20 minutes

Serving Size: 4 servings

Ingredients:

- 4 salmon fillets (6 ounces each), skin-on
- 1 cedar plank, soaked in water for at least 1 hour
- 2 tbsp. olive oil
- 2 tbsp. Dijon mustard
- 2 tbsp. honey
- 1 tbsp. chopped fresh dill
- Salt and pepper, to taste
- Lemon wedges, for serving

Instructions:

1. Preheat your Ninja woodfire outdoor grill and smoker to medium-high heat.
2. In a small bowl, whisk together the olive oil, Dijon mustard, honey, chopped dill, salt, and pepper to make a glaze.
3. Place the soaked cedar plank on the grill grates and close the lid for a few minutes to let it heat up.
4. Brush the skinless side of each salmon fillet with the glaze mixture.
5. Place the salmon fillets, skin-side down, on the preheated cedar plank.
6. Close the lid and grill for 15-20 minutes, or until the salmon is cooked through and flakes easily with a fork.
7. Remove from the grill, squeeze fresh lemon juice over the salmon, and serve.

Nutrition Information per Serving:

Calories: 350kcal | Fat: 20g | Protein: 35g | Carbohydrates: 10g | Fiber: 0g | Sugar: 9g | Sodium: 300mg

Cooking Tips:

- Soaking the cedar plank in water helps prevent it from burning during grilling and infuses the salmon with a pleasant smoky flavor.

- To check for doneness, gently insert a fork into the thickest part of the salmon and twist. If it flakes easily, it's done.

Grilled Ribeye Steak

Grill Time: 8-10 minutes

Serving Size: 2 servings

Ingredients:

- 2 ribeye steaks (1 inch thick), preferably bone-in
- 2 tbsp. olive oil
- 2 tsp. fresh rosemary, chopped
- Salt and pepper, to taste

Instructions

1. Preheat your Ninja woodfire outdoor grill and smoker to high heat.
2. In a small bowl, combine the olive oil, minced garlic, chopped rosemary, salt, and pepper.
3. Brush both sides of the ribeye steaks with the olive oil mixture.
4. Place the steaks on the preheated grill and cook for 4-5 minutes per side for medium-rare, or until desired doneness is reached.
5. Remove the steaks from the grill and let them rest for a few minutes before serving.

Nutrition Information per Serving:

Calories: 500kcal | Fat: 40g | Protein: 35g | Carbohydrates: 2g | Fiber: 0g | Sugar: 0g | Sodium: 100mg

Cooking Tips:

- Allow the steaks to come to room temperature before grilling for more even cooking.

- For perfect grill marks, resist the temptation to move the steaks around too much while grilling.

Smoked Whole Chicken

Grill Time: 2-3 hours

Serving Size: 4-6 servings

Ingredients:

- 1 whole chicken (3-4 pounds)
- 2 tbsp. olive oil
- 2 tsp. paprika
- 2 tsp. garlic powder
- 2 tsp. onion powder
- 1 tsp. dried thyme
- 1 tsp. dried oregano
- 1 tsp. salt

- ½ tsp. black pepper

Instructions:

1. Preheat your Ninja woodfire outdoor grill and smoker to 275°F (135°C).
2. Rinse the chicken under cold water and pat it dry with paper towels.
3. In a small bowl, combine the olive oil, paprika, garlic powder, onion powder, dried thyme, dried oregano, salt, and black pepper to make a spice rub.
4. Rub the spice mixture all over the chicken, including under the skin and inside the cavity.
5. Place the chicken on the smoker rack and smoke for 2-3 hours, or until the internal temperature reaches 165°F (74°C) in the thickest part of the thigh.
6. Remove the chicken from the smoker and let it rest for 10-15 minutes before carving.
7. Carve the chicken into serving pieces and serve.

Nutrition Information per serving (based on 6 servings):

Calories: 300kcal | Fat: 18g | Protein: 32g | Carbohydrates: 2g | Fiber: 2g | Sugar: 0g | Sodium: 400mg

Cooking Tips:

- To enhance the flavor, you can place a few sprigs of fresh herbs, such as rosemary or thyme, inside the cavity of the chicken before smoking.

- For crispy skin, you can increase the heat to 375°F (190°C) for the last 10-15 minutes of cooking after the chicken has reached the target internal temperature.

Grilled Shrimp Skewers

Grill Time: 6-8 minutes

Serving Size: 4 servings

Ingredients:

- 1 ½ pounds large shrimp, peeled and deveined
- 2 tbsp. olive oil
- 2 cloves garlic, minced
- 1 tsp. paprika
- ½ tsp. chili powder
- ½ tsp. dried oregano
- ½ tsp. salt
- ¼ tsp. black pepper
- Lemon wedges, for serving

Instructions:

1. Preheat your Ninja woodfire outdoor grill and smoker to medium-high heat.
2. In a bowl, combine the olive oil, minced garlic, paprika, chili powder, dried oregano, salt, and black pepper to make a marinade.
3. Add the shrimp to the marinade and toss to coat evenly. Let them marinate for 15-20 minutes.
4. Thread the shrimp onto skewers, leaving a small space between each shrimp.
5. Place the skewers on the preheated grill and cook for 3-4 minutes per side, or until the shrimp are opaque and cooked through.
6. Remove from the grill, squeeze fresh lemon juice over the shrimp, and serve.

Smoked Pork Ribs

Grill Time: 4-6 hours

Serving Size: 4 servings

Ingredients:

- 2 racks of pork ribs (about 4 pounds total)
- 2 tbsp. brown sugar
- 2 tsp. paprika
- 2 tsp. garlic powder
- 2 tsp. onion powder
- 1 tsp. chili powder
- 1 tsp. salt
- ½ tsp. black pepper
- Your favorite barbecue sauce

Instructions:

1. Preheat your Ninja woodfire outdoor grill and smoker to 225°F (107°C).
2. In a small bowl, combine the brown sugar, paprika, garlic powder, onion powder, chili powder, salt, and black pepper to make a dry rub.
3. Remove the silver skin from the back of the ribs if necessary.
4. Rub the dry rub all over the ribs, making sure to coat both sides.
5. Place the ribs on the smoker rack, bone side down, and smoke for 4-6 hours, or until the meat is tender and pulls away from the bone.

6. During the last 30 minutes of cooking, brush the ribs with your favorite barbecue sauce.

7. Remove the ribs from the smoker, let them rest for a few minutes, then slice and serve with extra barbecue sauce on the side.

Nutrition Information per Serving:

Calories: 600kcal | Fat: 40g | Protein: 50g | Carbohydrates: 8g | Fiber: 2g | Sugar: 6g | Sodium: 900mg

Cooking Tips:

- For more tender ribs, you can wrap them in foil after the first 2-3 hours of smoking and continue cooking until they are done.

- If you prefer a spicier flavor, you can add cayenne pepper or hot sauce to the dry rub.

Grilled Salmon with Lemon-Dill Sauce

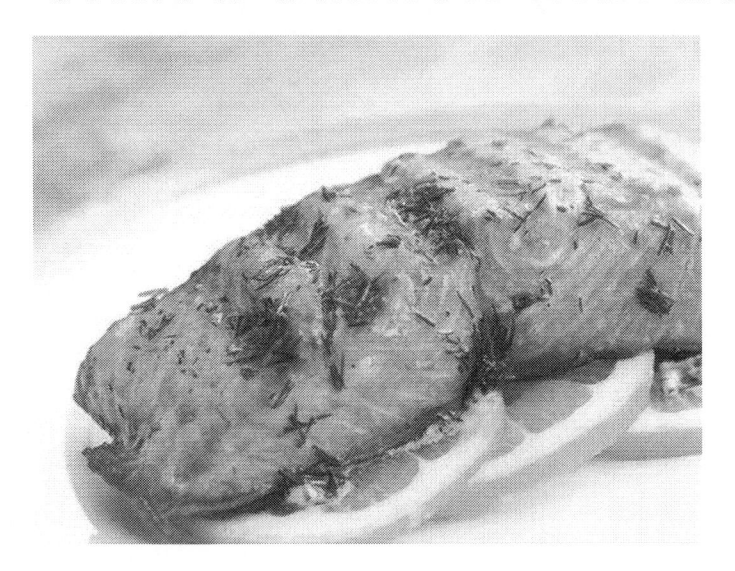

Grill Time: 10-12 minutes

Serving Size: 4 servings

Ingredients:

- 4 salmon fillets (6 ounces each)

- 2 tbsp. olive oil
- 2 tbsp. fresh lemon juice
- 2 cloves garlic, minced
- 1 tbsp. fresh dill, chopped
- Salt and pepper, to taste

Lemon-Dill Sauce:

- ½ cup mayonnaise
- 2 tbsp. fresh lemon juice
- 1 tbsp. fresh dill, chopped
- 1 tsp. Dijon mustard
- Salt and pepper, to taste

Instructions:

1. Preheat your Ninja woodfire outdoor grill and smoker to medium heat.
2. In a small bowl, whisk together the olive oil, lemon juice, minced garlic, chopped dill, salt, and pepper to make a marinade.
3. Place the salmon fillets in a shallow dish and pour the marinade over them. Let them marinate for 10-15 minutes.
4. In another bowl, whisk together the mayonnaise, lemon juice, chopped dill, Dijon mustard, salt, and pepper to make the lemon-dill sauce. Set aside.
5. Remove the salmon fillets from the marinade and place them on the preheated grill. Cook for 4-6 minutes per side, or until the fish flakes easily with a fork.
6. Remove the salmon from the grill and serve with the lemon-dill sauce on the side.

Nutrition Information per Serving:

Calories: 400kcal | Fat: 30g | Protein: 30g | Carbohydrates: 2g | Fiber: 0g | Sugar: 2g | Sodium: 400mg

Cooking Tips:

- To prevent the salmon from sticking to the grill, make sure it is well-oiled and preheated before placing the fish on it.

- If you prefer a stronger dill flavor, you can add more fresh dill to the marinade and the sauce.

Grilled Vegetable Skewers

Grill Time: 10-12 minutes

Serving Size: 4 servings

Ingredients:

- 2 zucchinis, sliced into rounds
- 1 red bell pepper, cut into chunks
- 1 yellow bell pepper, cut into chunks
- 1 red onion, cut into chunks
- 8-10 cherry tomatoes
- 2 tbsp. olive oil
- 2 cloves garlic, minced
- 1 tsp. dried oregano
- 1 tsp. dried basil
- Salt and pepper, to taste

Instructions:

1. Preheat your Ninja woodfire outdoor grill and smoker to medium-high heat.

2. In a bowl, combine the olive oil, minced garlic, dried oregano, dried basil, salt, and pepper to make a marinade.

3. Thread the vegetables onto skewers, alternating the different types of vegetables.

4. Brush the vegetable skewers with the marinade, making sure to coat them evenly.

5. Place the skewers on the preheated grill and cook for 4-6 minutes per side, or until the vegetables are tender and slightly charred.

6. Remove from the grill and serve as a side dish or with grilled meats.

Cooking Tips:

- Soak the wooden skewers in water for about 30 minutes before threading the vegetables to prevent them from burning on the grill.

- Feel free to customize the vegetable selection based on your preferences. Other great options include mushrooms, eggplant, and cherry tomatoes.

Smoked Beef Brisket

Grill Time: 10-12 hours

Serving Size: 8 servings

Ingredients:

- 8-10 pounds beef brisket, trimmed

- 2 tbsp. brown sugar

- 2 tbsp. paprika

- 2 tbsp. kosher salt

- 2 tsp. black pepper

- 2 tsp. garlic powder

- 2 tsp. onion powder
- 1 tsp. chili powder
- 1 tsp. dried thyme
- 1 tsp. dried oregano

Instructions:

1. Preheat your Ninja woodfire outdoor grill and smoker to 225°F (107°C).
2. In a bowl, combine the brown sugar, paprika, kosher salt, black pepper, garlic powder, onion powder, chili powder, dried thyme, and dried oregano to make a dry rub.
3. Rub the dry rub all over the beef brisket, making sure to coat all sides evenly.
4. Place the brisket on the smoker rack, fat side up, and smoke for 10-12 hours, or until the internal temperature reaches 195°F (90°C) and the meat is tender.
5. Remove the brisket from the smoker and let it rest for 30-45 minutes before slicing against the grain.
6. Serve the sliced brisket with your favorite barbecue sauce or as a sandwich with buns.

Cooking Tips:

- Brisket is a slow-cooking meat that benefits from low and slow heat. Maintain a consistent temperature throughout the smoking process for the best results.

- For added flavor, you can spritz the brisket with apple juice or beef broth every few hours while smoking.

Grilled Portobello Mushroom Burgers

Grill Time: 10-12 minutes

Serving Size: 4 servings

Ingredients:

- 4 large Portobello mushroom caps
- 4 hamburger buns
- 4 slices of Swiss or provolone cheese
- 4 tbsp. balsamic vinegar
- 2 tbsp. olive oil
- 2 cloves garlic, minced
- 1 tsp. dried thyme
- Salt and pepper, to taste
- Lettuce, tomato, and other burger toppings

Instructions:

1. Preheat your Ninja woodfire outdoor grill and smoker to medium heat.
2. In a small bowl, whisk together the balsamic vinegar, olive oil, minced garlic, dried thyme, salt, and pepper to make a marinade.
3. Remove the stems from the Portobello mushroom caps and brush both sides with the marinade.
4. Place the mushroom caps on the preheated grill and cook for 4-6 minutes per side, or until they are tender and slightly charred.

5. During the last minute of cooking, place a slice of cheese on top of each mushroom cap to melt.

6. Remove the mushroom caps from the grill and assemble the burgers with buns, lettuce, tomato, and any other desired toppings.

Cooking Tips:

- For a smokier flavor, you can add a small amount of wood chips or pellets to the grill while cooking the mushroom caps.

Grilled Salmon with Lemon Dill Sauce

Grill Time: 10-12 minutes

Serving Size: 4 servings

Ingredients:

- 4 salmon fillets
- 2 lemons, sliced
- 2 tbsp. olive oil
- Salt and pepper, to taste
- Fresh dill, chopped (for garnish)

Lemon Dill Sauce:

- ½ cup mayonnaise
- 1 tbsp. Dijon mustard
- 1 tbsp. lemon juice
- 1 tbsp. fresh dill, chopped
- Salt and pepper, to taste

Instructions:

1. Preheat your Ninja woodfire outdoor grill and smoker to medium-high heat.
2. Brush the salmon fillets with olive oil and season with salt and pepper.
3. Place the salmon fillets on the preheated grill, skin side down, and top each fillet with a couple of lemon slices.
4. Grill the salmon for 4-6 minutes per side, or until it flakes easily with a fork.
5. While the salmon is grilling, prepare the lemon dill sauce by whisking together the mayonnaise, Dijon mustard, lemon juice, fresh dill, salt, and pepper in a bowl.
6. Remove the grilled salmon from the grill and serve with a drizzle of lemon dill sauce and a sprinkle of fresh dill.

Cooking Tips:

- To prevent the salmon from sticking to the grill, make sure it is well-oiled and the grill grates are clean.

- Adjust the grilling time based on the thickness of the salmon fillets. Thicker fillets may require additional cooking time.

Chapter 5

Vibrant Grilled Side Dishes and Salad

Grilled Corn on the Cob

Grill Time: 10-15 minutes

Serving Size: 4 servings

Ingredients:

- 4 ears of corn, husks removed
- 2 tbsp. butter, melted
- Salt and pepper, to taste

Instructions:

1. Preheat your Ninja woodfire outdoor grill and smoker to medium heat.
2. Brush the ears of corn with melted butter and season with salt and pepper.
3. Place the corn directly on the grill grates and grill for 10-15 minutes, turning occasionally, until the corn is tender and lightly charred.
4. Remove from the grill and serve hot.

Cooking Tips:

- Soak the corn in water for about 15 minutes before grilling to prevent it from drying out.

- For added flavor, you can sprinkle the grilled corn with chili powder, paprika, or grated Parmesan cheese.

Grilled Asparagus

Grill Time: 8-10 minutes

Serving Size: 4 servings

Ingredients:

- 1 bunch asparagus, trimmed
- 2 tbsp. olive oil
- Salt and pepper, to taste
- Lemon wedges, for serving

Instructions:

1. Preheat your Ninja woodfire outdoor grill and smoker to medium-high heat.
2. Toss the asparagus spears with olive oil, salt, and pepper in a bowl until evenly coated.
3. Place the asparagus directly on the grill grates and grill for 8-10 minutes, turning occasionally, until the asparagus is tender and has grill marks.
4. Remove from the grill and serve with lemon wedges for squeezing over the asparagus.

Cooking Tips:

- To prevent the thin asparagus spears from falling through the grill grates, you can use a grilling basket or lay them perpendicular to the grates.

- Be mindful of the cooking time as asparagus can quickly become overcooked and lose its crispness.

Grilled Vegetable Salad

Grill Time: 15-20 minutes

Serving Size: 4 servings

Ingredients:

- 2 zucchinis, sliced lengthwise
- 2 yellow squash, sliced lengthwise
- 1 red bell pepper, seeded and quartered
- 1 red onion, sliced into rounds
- 1 cup cherry tomatoes
- 2 tbsp. balsamic vinegar
- 2 tbsp. olive oil
- 2 cloves garlic, minced
- 1 tsp. dried basil
- Salt and pepper, to taste
- Mixed salad greens

Instructions:

1. Preheat your Ninja woodfire outdoor grill and smoker to medium-high heat.
2. In a bowl, whisk together the balsamic vinegar, olive oil, minced garlic, dried basil, salt, and pepper to make a marinade.

3. Brush the zucchini, yellow squash, red bell pepper, and red onion with the marinade.

4. Place the vegetables on the preheated grill and cook for 3-4 minutes per side, or until they are tender and have grill marks.

5. Remove the grilled vegetables from the grill and let them cool slightly. Then, chop them into bite-sized pieces.

6. In a large bowl, combine the grilled vegetables, cherry tomatoes, and mixed salad greens. Drizzle with any remaining marinade and toss to coat.

7. Serve the grilled vegetable salad as a side dish or a light main course.

Cooking Tips:

- You can add other vegetables like eggplant, mushrooms, or asparagus to the salad based on your preferences.

- For added flavor, you can sprinkle the grilled vegetable salad with crumbled feta cheese or toasted pine nuts.

Smoked Macaroni and Cheese

Grill Time: 1 hour

Serving Size: 6 servings

Ingredients:

- 8 ounces elbow macaroni

- 2 cups shredded cheddar cheese

- 1 cup shredded mozzarella cheese

- 1 cup milk

- ¼ cup butter, melted

- 2 tbsp. all-purpose flour

- ½ tsp. garlic powder
- ½ tsp. onion powder
- ¼ tsp. smoked paprika
- Salt and pepper, to taste

Instructions:

1. Preheat your Ninja woodfire outdoor grill and smoker to 225°F (107°C).
2. Cook the elbow macaroni according to the package instructions until al dente. Drain and set aside.
3. In a saucepan, melt the butter over medium heat. Stir in the flour, garlic powder, onion powder, smoked paprika, salt, and pepper until well combined.
4. Gradually whisk in the milk, ensuring there are no lumps. Cook the mixture, stirring constantly, until it thickens and coats the back of a spoon.
5. Remove the saucepan from heat and stir in the shredded cheddar and mozzarella cheeses until melted and smooth.
6. In a large mixing bowl, combine the cooked macaroni with the cheese sauce. Stir until the macaroni is well coated.
7. Transfer the macaroni and cheese mixture to a cast iron skillet or a disposable aluminum pan.
8. Place the skillet or pan on the preheated grill and smoke for about 30-40 minutes, or until the top is golden brown and the cheese is bubbly.
9. Remove from the grill and let it cool for a few minutes before serving.

Cooking Tips:

- For a smokier flavor, you can add cooked and crumbled bacon or diced smoked sausage to the macaroni and cheese before smoking it.

- If you prefer a more traditional baked macaroni and cheese, you can transfer the mixture to a baking dish and bake it in a preheated oven at 375°F (190°C) for about 20-25 minutes instead of smoking it.

Grilled Watermelon Salad

Grill Time: 10 minutes

Serving Size: 4 servings

Ingredients:

- 4 thick slices of watermelon, rind removed
- 4 cups arugula or mixed salad greens
- ½ cup crumbled feta cheese
- ¼ cup sliced red onions
- ¼ cup chopped fresh mint leaves
- 2 tbsp. balsamic glaze
- 2 tbsp. olive oil
- Salt and pepper, to taste

Instructions:

1. Preheat your Ninja woodfire outdoor grill and smoker to medium-high heat.
2. Brush the watermelon slices with olive oil and season with salt and pepper.
3. Place the watermelon slices directly on the grill grates and grill for about 2-3 minutes per side, or until grill marks appear.
4. Remove the grilled watermelon slices from the grill and let them cool slightly. Then, cut them into bite-sized cubes.
5. In a large bowl, combine the arugula or mixed salad greens, grilled watermelon cubes, crumbled feta cheese, sliced red onions, and chopped mint leaves.
6. Drizzle the salad with balsamic glaze and olive oil. Season with salt and pepper, and toss gently to combine.
7. Serve the grilled watermelon salad immediately.

Cooking Tips:

- You can add other ingredients like cherry tomatoes, cucumber slices, or toasted pine nuts to the salad for extra flavor and texture.

- If you don't have balsamic glaze, you can drizzle the salad with a mixture of balsamic vinegar and honey.

Smoked Potato Salad

Grill Time: 1 hour 30 minutes

Serving Size: 6 servings

Ingredients:

- 6 medium-sized potatoes, peeled and cubed
- ½ cup mayonnaise
- ¼ cup sour cream
- 2 tbsp. Dijon mustard
- 2 tbsp. apple cider vinegar
- 1 tbsp. chopped fresh dill
- 1 tbsp. chopped fresh parsley
- ½ tsp. garlic powder

- Salt and pepper, to taste
- 4 hard-boiled eggs, peeled and chopped
- ¼ cup chopped red onions
- ¼ cup chopped celery

Instructions:

1. Preheat your Ninja woodfire outdoor grill and smoker to 225°F (107°C).
2. Place the cubed potatoes in a disposable aluminum pan or a cast iron skillet.
3. Place the pan or skillet on the preheated grill and smoke the potatoes for about 1 hour, or until they are tender and lightly browned, stirring occasionally.
4. In a large mixing bowl, whisk together the mayonnaise, sour cream, Dijon mustard, apple cider vinegar, chopped dill, chopped parsley, garlic powder, salt, and pepper.
5. Add the smoked potatoes, chopped hard-boiled eggs, chopped red onions, and chopped celery to the bowl. Gently toss until all the ingredients are well coated with the dressing.
6. Cover the bowl and refrigerate the potato salad for at least 1 hour before serving.

Cooking Tips:

- You can add crispy cooked bacon or pickle relish to the potato salad for additional flavor.

- For a creamier texture, you can increase the amount of mayonnaise and sour cream in the dressing.

Grilled Caesar Salad

Grill Time: 10 minutes

Serving Size: 4 servings

Ingredients:

- 2 romaine lettuce hearts, halved lengthwise
- 2 tbsp. olive oil
- Salt and pepper, to taste
- Caesar dressing
- Grated Parmesan cheese
- Croutons

Instructions:

1. Preheat your Ninja woodfire outdoor grill and smoker to medium-high heat.
2. Brush the cut sides of the romaine lettuce hearts with olive oil and season with salt and pepper.
3. Place the lettuce halves directly on the grill grates, cut side down, and grill for about 2-3 minutes, or until lightly charred.
4. Remove the grilled lettuce halves from the grill and let them cool slightly. Then, chop them into bite-sized pieces.
5. In a large bowl, combine the chopped grilled lettuce, Caesar dressing, grated Parmesan cheese, and croutons. Toss gently to coat the lettuce with the dressing.
6. Serve the grilled Caesar salad immediately.

Cooking Tips:

- To add a smoky flavor to the Caesar dressing, you can whisk in a small amount of liquid smoke or smoked paprika.

- For extra crunch, you can make homemade croutons by tossing cubed bread with olive oil, salt, and pepper, and toasting them on the grill until golden brown.

Smoked Baked Beans

Grill Time: 2 hours

Serving Size: 8 servings

Ingredients:

- 4 cans (15 ounces each) of canned baked beans
- ½ cup barbecue sauce
- ¼ cup brown sugar
- 2 tbsp. yellow mustard
- 1 small onion, finely chopped
- 4 slices cooked bacon, crumbled
- Salt and pepper, to taste

Instructions:

1. Preheat your Ninja woodfire outdoor grill and smoker to 225°F (107°C).
2. In a large disposable aluminum pan or a cast iron skillet, combine the canned baked beans, barbecue sauce, brown sugar, yellow mustard, chopped onion, and crumbled bacon. Stir well to combine.
3. Place the pan or skillet on the preheated grill and smoke the beans for about 1.5 to 2 hours, stirring occasionally, until the flavors meld together.
4. Season with salt and pepper to taste, and serve hot.

Cooking Tips:

- For a smokier flavor, you can add diced smoked sausage or pulled pork to the baked beans before smoking.

- If you prefer sweeter baked beans, you can increase the amount of brown sugar or add a tbsp. of molasses to the mixture.

Grilled Vegetable Skewers

Grill Time: 10-15 minutes

Serving Size: 4 servings

Ingredients:

- 1 zucchini, sliced into rounds

- 1 yellow squash, sliced into rounds

- 1 red bell pepper, seeded and cut into chunks

- 1 red onion, cut into chunks

- 8-10 cherry tomatoes

- 2 tbsp. olive oil

- 2 cloves garlic, minced

- 1 tsp. dried Italian seasoning

- Salt and pepper, to taste

Instructions:

1. Preheat your Ninja woodfire outdoor grill and smoker to medium-high heat.
2. In a bowl, combine the olive oil, minced garlic, dried Italian seasoning, salt, and pepper.

3. Thread the zucchini rounds, yellow squash rounds, red bell pepper chunks, red onion chunks, and cherry tomatoes onto skewers, alternating the vegetables.

4. Brush the vegetable skewers with the olive oil mixture.

5. Place the skewers directly on the grill grates and grill for 10-15 minutes, turning occasionally, until the vegetables are tender and lightly charred.

6. Remove from the grill and serve hot.

Cooking Tips:

- If using wooden skewers, make sure to soak them in water for about 30 minutes before threading the vegetables to prevent them from burning.

- You can customize the vegetable skewers by adding mushrooms, eggplant, or other favorite vegetables.

Grilled Caprese Salad Skewers

Grill Time: 10 minutes

Serving Size: 4 servings

Ingredients:

- 8-10 cherry tomatoes
- 8-10 small fresh mozzarella balls
- Fresh basil leaves
- 2 tbsp. balsamic glaze
- 2 tbsp. olive oil
- Salt and pepper, to taste

Instructions:

1. Preheat your Ninja woodfire outdoor grill and smoker to medium-high heat.

2. Thread a cherry tomato, a fresh mozzarella ball, and a basil leaf onto each skewer, repeating until all ingredients are used.

3. In a small bowl, whisk together the balsamic glaze, olive oil, salt, and pepper.

4. Brush the skewers with the balsamic glaze mixture.

5. Place the skewers directly on the grill grates and grill for about 2-3 minutes per side, or until the cheese begins to melt and the tomatoes are slightly charred.

6. Remove from the grill and drizzle with additional balsamic glaze if desired.

7. Serve the grilled Caprese salad skewers warm.

Cooking Tips:

- If you don't have balsamic glaze, you can make a simple balsamic reduction by simmering balsamic vinegar in a small saucepan until it thickens and reduces in volume.

- Feel free to add a sprinkle of freshly ground black pepper or a drizzle of olive oil over the finished skewers for added flavor.

Chapter 6

Smoky Grilled Seafood Options

Grilled Shrimp Tacos with Lime Slaw

Grill Time: Approximately 15 minutes

Serving Size: 4 servings

Ingredients:

- 1 pound large shrimp, peeled and deveined
- 2 tbsp. olive oil
- 2 cloves garlic, minced
- 1 tsp. chili powder
- ½ tsp. cumin
- Salt and pepper to taste
- 8 small flour tortillas
- Lime wedges, for serving

For the Lime Slaw:

- 2 cups shredded cabbage

- ¼ cup mayonnaise
- 1 tbsp. lime juice
- 1 tsp. honey
- Salt and pepper to taste

Instructions:

1. Preheat the grill to medium-high heat.
2. In a bowl, combine olive oil, minced garlic, chili powder, cumin, salt, and pepper to make the marinade.
3. Add the shrimp to the marinade and toss until they are well coated.
4. Thread the marinated shrimp onto skewers.
5. Place the shrimp skewers on the preheated grill and cook for about 2-3 minutes per side or until the shrimp are pink and cooked through.
6. While the shrimp are grilling, prepare the lime slaw by combining shredded cabbage, mayonnaise, lime juice, honey, salt, and pepper in a bowl. Toss until well coated.
7. Warm the flour tortillas on the grill for about 30 seconds on each side.
8. Remove the shrimp skewers from the grill and let them rest for a minute.
9. To assemble the tacos, place a scoop of lime slaw on each warmed tortilla and top with grilled shrimp. Squeeze lime juice over the tacos. Serve hot with additional lime wedges on the side.

Nutrition Information (per serving):

Calories: 350 | Fat: 15g | Carbohydrates: 30g | Protein: 25g

Smoked Salmon with Dill Sauce

Grill Time: 1-2 hours

Serving Size: 4 servings

Ingredients:

- 1 pound salmon fillet
- 2 tbsp. olive oil
- Salt and pepper, to taste
- 1 tbsp. fresh dill, chopped
- 2 tbsp. Greek yogurt
- 1 tbsp. lemon juice
- Lemon slices, for serving

Instructions:

1. Preheat your Ninja woodfire outdoor grill and smoker to 225°F (107°C).
2. Rub the salmon fillet with olive oil and season it with salt and pepper.
3. Place the salmon directly on the grill grates, skin-side down.
4. Close the lid and smoke the salmon for 1-2 hours, or until it reaches an internal temperature of 145°F (63°C).
5. In a small bowl, mix together the fresh dill, Greek yogurt, and lemon juice to make the dill sauce.
6. Serve the smoked salmon with the dill sauce and lemon slices.

Nutrition Information per Serving:

Calories: 237 | Protein: 25g | Fat: 14g | Carbohydrates: 2g | Fiber: 0g

Cooking Tips:

- Use a smoker box or wood chips to infuse smoky flavor into the salmon.

- Let the salmon rest for a few minutes after smoking to allow the flavors to develop.

Grilled Teriyaki Tuna Steaks

Grill Time: 6-8 minutes

Serving Size: 4 servings

Ingredients:

- 4 tuna steaks (6-8 ounces each)
- ¼ cup soy sauce
- 2 tbsp. honey
- 1 tbsp. rice vinegar
- 1 tbsp. sesame oil
- 2 cloves garlic, minced
- 1 tsp. grated fresh ginger

- Sesame seeds, for garnish
- Green onions, sliced, for garnish

Instructions:

1. Preheat your Ninja woodfire outdoor grill and smoker to medium-high heat.
2. In a bowl, whisk together the soy sauce, honey, rice vinegar, sesame oil, minced garlic, and grated ginger to make the teriyaki marinade.
3. Place the tuna steaks in a shallow dish and pour the marinade over them, reserving a small amount for basting.
4. Let the tuna marinate for 15-30 minutes.
5. Remove the tuna steaks from the marinade and grill for 3-4 minutes per side, basting with the reserved marinade.
6. Remove from the grill and sprinkle with sesame seeds and sliced green onions.
7. Serve hot.

Grilled Lemon Garlic Shrimp Skewers

Grill Time: 8-10 minutes

Serving Size: 4 servings

Ingredients:

- 1 pound large shrimp, peeled and deveined
- 2 tbsp. olive oil
- 3 cloves garlic, minced
- 2 tbsp. fresh lemon juice
- 1 tsp. lemon zest
- ½ tsp. smoked paprika
- Salt and pepper, to taste
- Fresh parsley, for garnish

Instructions:

1. Preheat your Ninja woodfire outdoor grill and smoker to medium-high heat.
2. In a bowl, combine the olive oil, minced garlic, lemon juice, lemon zest, smoked paprika, salt, and pepper.
3. Thread the shrimp onto skewers, dividing them evenly.
4. Brush the shrimp skewers with the marinade mixture.
5. Place the skewers directly on the grill grates and grill for 4-5 minutes per side, or until the shrimp are opaque and cooked through.
6. Remove from the grill and garnish with fresh parsley.
7. Serve hot.

Nutrition Information per Serving:

Calories: 168 | Protein: 23g | Fat: 7g | Carbohydrates: 2g | Fiber: 0g

Cooking Tips:

- Soak wooden skewers in water for about 30 minutes before threading the shrimp to prevent them from burning.

- Marinate the shrimp for 15-30 minutes before grilling to enhance the flavor.

Grilled Garlic Butter Lobster Tails

Grill Time: 8-10 minutes

Serving Size: 2 servings

Ingredients:

- 2 lobster tails
- 4 tbsp. unsalted butter, melted
- 2 cloves garlic, minced
- 1 tbsp. fresh lemon juice
- Salt and pepper, to taste
- Fresh parsley, for garnish

Instructions:

1. Preheat your Ninja woodfire outdoor grill and smoker to medium-high heat.
2. Using kitchen shears, cut the top shell of each lobster tail lengthwise, exposing the meat.
3. Carefully lift the meat through the cut shell, keeping it attached at the base, and place it on top of the shell.
4. In a small bowl, combine the melted butter, minced garlic, lemon juice, salt, and pepper.
5. Brush the garlic butter mixture over the lobster tails.
6. Place the lobster tails directly on the grill grates and grill for 4-5 minutes per side, or until the meat is opaque and cooked through.
7. Remove from the grill and garnish with fresh parsley.
8. Serve hot with additional garlic butter on the side.

Nutrition Information per Serving:

Calories: 289 | Protein: 32g | Fat: 17g | Carbohydrates: 2g | Fiber: 0g

Cooking Tips:

- To prevent the lobster tails from curling while grilling, you can insert a skewer through the length of each tail.

- Baste the lobster tails with the garlic butter mixture while grilling to keep them moist and flavorful.

Cedar Plank Grilled Salmon

Grill Time: 12-15 minutes

Serving Size: 4 servings

Ingredients:

- 4 salmon fillets (6 ounces each)
- Cedar planks, soaked in water for at least 1 hour
- 2 tbsp. olive oil
- 2 tbsp. Dijon mustard
- 2 tbsp. maple syrup
- 1 tsp. smoked paprika
- Salt and pepper, to taste
- Fresh dill, for garnish

Instructions:

1. Preheat your Ninja woodfire outdoor grill and smoker to medium-high heat.
2. In a small bowl, whisk together the olive oil, Dijon mustard, maple syrup, smoked paprika, salt, and pepper to make the marinade.
3. Place the salmon fillets in a shallow dish and pour the marinade over them, coating all sides.

4. Remove the cedar planks from the water and place the marinated salmon fillets directly on top of the planks.

5. Place the cedar planks with the salmon on the grill grates and close the lid.

6. Grill for 12-15 minutes, or until the salmon is cooked to your desired doneness.

7. Remove from the grill and garnish with fresh dill.

8. Serve hot.

Nutrition Information per Serving:

Calories: 346 | Protein: 34g | Fat: 22g | Carbohydrates: 7g | Fiber: 0g

Cooking Tips:

- Soaking the cedar planks in water helps prevent them from burning while grilling and imparts a smoky flavor to the salmon.

- Place the cedar planks on the grill for a few minutes before adding the salmon to preheat them and enhance the smoky flavor.

Grilled Cajun Shrimp Tacos

Grill Time: 6-8 minutes

Serving Size: 4 servings

Ingredients:

- 1 pound large shrimp, peeled and deveined
- 2 tbsp. olive oil
- 1 tbsp. Cajun seasoning
- 1 tsp. paprika
- ½ tsp. garlic powder
- ½ tsp. onion powder

- ¼ tsp. cayenne pepper (optional, for extra heat)
- Salt and pepper, to taste
- 8 small tortillas (corn or flour)
- Shredded lettuce, for serving
- Diced tomatoes, for serving
- Sliced avocado, for serving
- Cilantro, for garnish
- Lime wedges, for serving

Instructions:

1. Preheat your Ninja woodfire outdoor grill and smoker to medium-high heat.
2. In a bowl, combine the olive oil, Cajun seasoning, paprika, garlic powder, onion powder, cayenne pepper (if using), salt and pepper. Mix well to form a marinade.
3. Add the shrimp to the marinade and toss to coat evenly. Let it marinate for about 15 minutes.
4. Thread the shrimp onto skewers, leaving a little space between each shrimp.
5. Place the shrimp skewers on the preheated grill and cook for 3-4 minutes per side, or until the shrimp are pink and opaque.
6. While the shrimp are cooking, warm the tortillas on the grill for about 30 seconds per side.
7. Remove the shrimp from the skewers and divide them among the tortillas.
8. Top the shrimp with shredded lettuce, diced tomatoes, sliced avocado, and cilantro.
9. Squeeze fresh lime juice over the tacos. Serve hot and enjoy!

Nutrition Information per Serving:

Calories: 316| Protein: 27g| Fat: 12g| Carbohydrates: 24g| Fiber: 4g

Cooking Tips:

- If using wooden skewers, make sure to soak them in water for about 30 minutes before threading the shrimp to prevent them from burning on the grill.

- Feel free to adjust the amount of Cajun seasoning and cayenne pepper according to your desired level of spiciness.

Grilled Teriyaki Glazed Salmon Skewers

Grill Time: 10-12 minutes

Serving Size: 4 servings

Ingredients:

- 1.5 pounds salmon fillets, skin removed, cut into 1-inch cubes
- ¼ cup soy sauce
- 2 tbsp. honey
- 2 tbsp. rice vinegar
- 1 tbsp. sesame oil
- 2 cloves garlic, minced
- 1 tsp. grated ginger
- 1 tbsp. cornstarch
- ¼ cup water
- Sliced green onions, for garnish
- Sesame seeds, for garnish

Instructions:

1. Preheat your Ninja woodfire outdoor grill and smoker to medium-high heat.
2. In a bowl, whisk together the soy sauce, honey, rice vinegar, sesame oil, minced garlic, and grated ginger to make the teriyaki sauce.

3. In a small saucepan, combine the cornstarch and water, stir until smooth. Add the teriyaki sauce to the saucepan and cook over medium heat until the sauce thickens, stirring constantly. Remove from heat.

4. Thread the salmon cubes onto skewers and brush them generously with the teriyaki glaze.

5. Place the salmon skewers on the preheated grill and cook for 4-5 minutes per side, or until the salmon is cooked through and slightly charred on the edges.

6. Remove from the grill and garnish with sliced green onions and sesame seeds.

7. Serve hot with extra teriyaki glaze on the side.

Nutrition Information per Serving:

Calories: 330| Protein: 35g| Fat: 13g| Carbohydrates: 17g| Fiber: 0g

Cooking Tips:

- Soaking wooden skewers in water for about 30 minutes before threading the salmon will help prevent them from burning on the grill.

- Baste the salmon skewers with the teriyaki glaze while grilling to enhance the flavor.

Grilled Garlic Herb Shrimp Skewers

Grill Time: 6-8 minutes

Serving Size: 4 servings

Ingredients:

- 1.5 pounds large shrimp, peeled and deveined

- 2 tbsp. olive oil

- 2 cloves garlic, minced

- 1 tbsp. fresh lemon juice

- 1 tbsp. chopped fresh parsley

- 1 tbsp. chopped fresh basil

- 1 tsp. chopped fresh thyme

- Salt and pepper, to taste

- Lemon wedges, for serving

Instructions:

1. Preheat your Ninja woodfire outdoor grill and smoker to medium-high heat.
2. In a bowl, combine the olive oil, minced garlic, lemon juice, chopped parsley, basil, thyme, salt, and pepper to make the marinade.
3. Add the shrimp to the marinade and toss to coat evenly. Let it marinate for about 15 minutes.
4. Thread the marinated shrimp onto skewers, leaving a little space between each shrimp.
5. Place the shrimp skewers on the preheated grill and cook for 2-3 minutes per side, or until the shrimp turn pink and opaque.
6. Remove from the grill and squeeze fresh lemon juice over the shrimp skewers.
7. Serve hot with lemon wedges.

Nutrition Information per Serving:

Calories: 200 | Protein: 30g | Fat: 8g | Carbohydrates: 2g | Fiber: 0g

Cooking Tips:

- If using wooden skewers, soak them in water for about 30 minutes before threading the shrimp to prevent them from burning on the grill.

- Feel free to customize the herb selection based on your preferences. You can also add a pinch of red pepper flakes for a hint of spice.

Grilled Sesame Ginger Tuna Steaks

Grill Time: 4-6 minutes

Serving Size: 4 servings

Ingredients:

- 4 tuna steaks (6 ounces each)

- 2 tbsp. soy sauce

- 2 tbsp. sesame oil

- 1 tbsp. honey

- 1 tbsp. grated ginger

- 1 tbsp. rice vinegar

- 2 cloves garlic, minced

- 1 tbsp. sesame seeds

- Sliced green onions, for garnish

Instructions:

1. Preheat your Ninja woodfire outdoor grill and smoker to high heat.
2. In a bowl, whisk together the soy sauce, sesame oil, honey, grated ginger, rice vinegar, minced garlic, and sesame seeds to make the marinade.
3. Place the tuna steaks in a shallow dish and pour the marinade over them, coating all sides. Let them marinate for about 15-30 minutes.
4. Remove the tuna steaks from the marinade, reserving the marinade for basting.

5. Place the tuna steaks on the preheated grill and cook for 2-3 minutes per side for medium-rare, or adjust the cooking time according to your desired level of doneness.

6. While grilling, brush the tuna steaks with the reserved marinade to enhance the flavor.

7. Remove from the grill and garnish with sliced green onions.

8. Serve hot.

Nutrition Information per Serving:

Calories: 304 | Protein: 42g| Fat: 12g| Carbohydrates: 5g| Fiber: 2g

Cooking Tips:

- Tuna steaks are best when cooked to medium-rare or medium to maintain their tenderness and juiciness.

- Use a basting brush to coat the tuna steaks with the marinade while grilling for additional flavor.

Smoked Maple Glazed Cedar Plank Salmon

Grill Time: 20-25 minutes

Serving Size: 4 servings

Ingredients:

1. 1 cedar plank, soaked in water for at least 1 hour
2. 1.5 pounds salmon fillet, skin on
3. ¼ cup maple syrup
4. 2 tbsp. Dijon mustard
5. 1 tbsp. soy sauce
6. 1 tbsp. apple cider vinegar
7. 1 tsp. smoked paprika
8. Salt and pepper, to taste
9. Fresh dill, for garnish
10. Lemon wedges, for serving

Instructions:

1. Preheat your Ninja woodfire outdoor grill and smoker to medium heat.
2. In a small bowl, whisk together the maple syrup, Dijon mustard, soy sauce, apple cider vinegar, smoked paprika, salt, and pepper to make the glaze.
3. Place the soaked cedar plank on the grill and close the lid. Let it preheat for about 5 minutes.

4. Season the salmon fillet with salt and pepper on both sides. Place the salmon, skin side down, on the preheated cedar plank.

5. Brush the salmon generously with the maple glaze, reserving some for basting.

6. Close the lid of the grill and smoke the salmon for 15-20 minutes, or until it reaches your desired level of doneness.

7. While smoking, baste the salmon with the remaining maple glaze every 5 minutes.

8. Remove the cedar plank from the grill and let it rest for a few minutes.

9. Garnish with fresh dill and serve with lemon wedges.

Nutrition Information per Serving:

Calories: 350 | Protein: 34gF | at: 19g | Carbohydrates: 12g | Fiber: 0g

Cooking Tips:

- Soaking the cedar plank in water prevents it from catching fire and adds a subtle smoky flavor to the salmon.

- Make sure to keep an eye on the salmon while smoking to prevent overcooking.

Grilled Coconut Lime Shrimp Skewers

Grill Time: 4-6 minutes

Serving Size: 4 servings

Ingredients:

- 1½ pounds large shrimp, peeled and deveined
- ½ cup coconut milk
- Zest and juice of 2 limes
- 2 tbsp. chopped fresh cilantro
- 1 tbsp. honey

- 1 tbsp. soy sauce
- 2 cloves garlic, minced
- 1 tsp. grated ginger
- Salt and pepper, to taste
- Lime wedges, for serving

Instructions:

1. Preheat your Ninja woodfire outdoor grill and smoker to medium-high heat.
2. In a bowl, combine the coconut milk, lime zest, lime juice, chopped cilantro, honey, soy sauce, minced garlic, grated ginger, salt, and pepper to make the marinade.
3. Add the shrimp to the marinade and toss to coat evenly. Let it marinate for about 15 minutes.
4. Thread the marinated shrimp onto skewers, leaving a little space between each shrimp.
5. Place the shrimp skewers on the preheated grill and cook for 2-3 minutes per side, or until the shrimp turn pink and opaque.
6. Remove from the grill and squeeze fresh lime juice over the shrimp skewers.
7. Serve hot with lime wedges.

Nutrition Information per Serving:

Calories: 220 | Protein: 24g | Fat: 9g | Carbohydrates: 10g | Fiber: 0g

Cooking Tips:

- If using wooden skewers, soak them in water for about 30 minutes before threading the shrimp to prevent them from burning on the grill.

- For an extra touch of flavor, sprinkle the grilled shrimp skewers with additional chopped cilantro before serving.

Grilled Cajun Blackened Red Snapper

Grill Time: 8-10 minutes

Serving Size: 4 servings

Ingredients:

- 4 red snapper fillets (6 ounces each), skin on
- 2 tbsp. olive oil
- 2 tbsp. Cajun seasoning
- 1 tsp. paprika
- ½ tsp. garlic powder
- ½ tsp. dried thyme
- ½ tsp. dried oregano
- Salt, to taste
- Salt, to taste
- Fresh lemon wedges, for serving

Instructions:

1. Preheat your Ninja woodfire outdoor grill and smoker to medium-high heat.
2. In a small bowl, combine the Cajun seasoning, paprika, garlic powder, dried thyme, dried oregano, and salt.
3. Pat dry the red snapper fillets with a paper towel. Brush both sides of the fillets with olive oil.
4. Sprinkle the Cajun spice mixture evenly over the fillets, pressing it gently to adhere.
5. Place the seasoned red snapper fillets on the preheated grill, skin side down.
6. Grill the fillets for 4-5 minutes per side, or until the flesh is opaque and flakes easily with a fork.

7. Remove from the grill and serve hot with fresh lemon wedges.

Nutrition Information per Serving:

Calories: 240 | Protein: 36g | Fat: 9g | Carbohydrates: 2g | Fiber: 0g

Cooking Tips:

- Adjust the amount of Cajun seasoning according to your spice preference.

- To prevent the fish from sticking to the grill, make sure the grill grates are clean and well-oiled before cooking.

Chapter 7

Creative Grilled Pizza & Flatbread

Grilled Veggie Flatbread with Pesto

Grill Time: 15-20 minutes

Serving Size: 2-4 people

Ingredients:

- Flatbread or naan bread
- ¼ cup pesto sauce
- 1 cup mixed grilled vegetables (bell peppers, zucchini, and eggplant), sliced
- ½ cup shredded mozzarella cheese
- Fresh basil leaves for garnish
- Salt and pepper to taste

Instructions:

1. Preheat your Ninja Woodfire Outdoor Grill and Smoker to medium heat.
2. Spread the pesto sauce evenly on the flatbread.
3. Arrange the grilled vegetables on top of the pesto.
4. Sprinkle the shredded mozzarella cheese over the vegetables.
5. Season with salt and pepper to taste.
6. Carefully transfer the flatbread onto the grill grates.
7. Close the lid and cook for 5-8 minutes or until the cheese has MELTED and the edges are crispy.
8. Remove the flatbread from the grill and let it cool for a minute.
9. Garnish with fresh basil leaves. Slice and serve warm.

Nutrition Information (per serving):

- Calories: 250
- Fat: 10g
- Carbohydrates: 30g
- Protein: 12g

Cooking Tips:

- Preheat your grill and smoker to ensure even cooking and to prevent the flatbread from sticking to the grates.

- Grilling the vegetables before adding them to the flatbread adds a smoky flavor and enhances their natural sweetness.

- Experiment with different pesto varieties, such as basil pesto or sun-dried tomato pesto, to create different flavor profiles.

BBQ Pulled Pork Pizza

Grill Time: Approximately 15-20 minutes

Serving Size: 2-4 people

Ingredients:

- Pizza dough (store-bought or homemade)

- ½ cup barbecue sauce

- 1 cup cooked pulled pork

- ¼ cup red onion, thinly sliced

- 1 cup shredded mozzarella cheese

- Fresh cilantro leaves for garnish

- Salt and pepper to taste

Instructions:

1. Preheat your Ninja Woodfire Outdoor Grill and Smoker to medium-high heat.
2. Roll out the pizza dough on a floured surface to your desired thickness.
3. Place the rolled-out dough on a pizza peel or a floured baking sheet.
4. Spread barbecue sauce evenly over the dough, leaving a small border around the edges.
5. Arrange the pulled pork and red onion slices on top of the sauce.
6. Sprinkle the shredded mozzarella cheese over the toppings.
7. Season with salt and pepper to taste.
8. Carefully transfer the pizza from the peel or baking sheet onto the preheated grill grates.
9. Close the lid and cook for 8-10 minutes or until the crust is golden brown and the cheese has melted.
10. Remove the pizza from the grill and let it cool for a few minutes.
11. Garnish with fresh cilantro leaves.
12. Slice and serve hot.

Nutrition Information (per serving):

- Calories: 320
- Fat: 12g
- Carbohydrates: 35g
- Protein: 18g

Cooking Tips:

- Use leftover cooked pulled pork or prepare it in advance for this recipe. Slow-cooked, tender pulled pork works best for maximum flavor.
- Brush the pizza dough with a little olive oil before adding the toppings to prevent it from becoming soggy.

- For an added kick, drizzle a small amount of additional barbecue sauce on top of the pizza before serving.

Grilled Mediterranean Flatbread

Grill Time: Approximately 15-20 minutes

Serving Size: 2-4 people

Ingredients:

- Flatbread or naan bread

- ¼ cup hummus

- ½ cup cherry tomatoes, halved

- ¼ cup Kalamata olives, sliced

- ¼ cup red onion, thinly sliced

- ¼ cup crumbled feta cheese

- Fresh parsley leaves for garnish

- Salt and pepper to taste

Instructions:

1. Preheat your Ninja Woodfire Outdoor Grill and Smoker to medium heat.

2. Spread the hummus evenly on the flatbread.

3. Arrange the cherry tomatoes, Kalamata olives, and red onion slices on top of the hummus.

4. Sprinkle the crumbled feta cheese over the toppings.

5. Season with salt and pepper to taste.

6. Carefully transfer the flatbread onto the grill grates.

7. Close the lid and cook for 5-8 minutes or until the edges are crispy and the toppings are warmed through.

8. Remove the flatbread from the grill and let it cool for a minute.

9. Garnish with fresh parsley leaves.

10. Slice and serve warm.

Nutrition Information (per serving):

- Calories: 220

- Fat: 8g

- Carbohydrates: 30g

- Protein: 8g

Cooking Tips:

- You can use traditional hummus or experiment with different flavors like roasted red pepper or garlic hummus for added variety.

- For a smoky twist, grill the cherry tomatoes for a few minutes before adding them to the flatbread.

- Serve with a side of tzatziki sauce for dipping.

Thai Chicken Pizza

Grill Time: Approximately 15-20 minutes

Serving Size: 2-4 people

Ingredients:

- Pizza dough (store-bought or homemade)

- ¼ cup peanut sauce

- 1 cup cooked chicken, shredded

- ¼ cup red bell pepper, thinly sliced

- ¼ cup carrot, julienned

- ¼ cup cilantro leaves, chopped

- Crushed peanuts for garnish

- Salt and pepper to taste

Instructions:

1. Preheat your Ninja Woodfire Outdoor Grill and Smoker to medium-high heat.

2. Roll out the pizza dough on a floured surface to your desired thickness.

3. Place the rolled-out dough on a pizza peel or a floured baking sheet.

4. Spread peanut sauce evenly over the dough, leaving a small border around the edges.

5. Arrange the shredded chicken, red bell pepper, and carrot on top of the sauce.

6. Season with salt and pepper to taste.

7. Carefully transfer the pizza from the peel or baking sheet onto the preheated grill grates.

8. Close the lid and cook for 8-10 minutes or until the crust is golden brown and the toppings are heated through.

9. Remove the pizza from the grill and let it cool for a few minutes.

10. Garnish with cilantro leaves and crushed peanuts.

11. Slice and serve hot.

Nutrition Information (per serving):

- Calories: 280

- Fat: 10g

- Carbohydrates: 30g

- Protein: 18g

Cooking Tips:

- Use leftover cooked chicken or grill chicken breasts beforehand and shred them for this recipe.

- Drizzle a little additional peanut sauce on top of the pizza before serving for an extra burst of flavor.

- If you prefer a spicier kick, add some sliced Thai chili peppers or a drizzle of sriracha sauce.

Caprese Grilled Pizza

Grill Time: Approximately 15-20 minutes

Serving Size: 2-4 people

Ingredients:

- Pizza dough (store-bought or homemade)
- ¼ cup tomato sauce
- 8 ounces fresh mozzarella cheese, sliced
- 1 cup cherry tomatoes, halved
- Fresh basil leaves
- Balsamic glaze for drizzling
- Salt and pepper to taste

Instructions:

1. Preheat your Ninja Woodfire Outdoor Grill and Smoker to medium-high heat.

2. Roll out the pizza dough on a floured surface to your desired thickness.

3. Place the rolled-out dough on a pizza peel or a floured baking sheet.

4. Spread tomato sauce evenly over the dough, leaving a small border around the edges.

5. Arrange the mozzarella slices and cherry tomato halves on top of the sauce.

6. Season with salt and pepper to taste.

7. Carefully transfer the pizza from the peel or baking sheet onto the preheated grill grates.

8. Close the lid and cook for 8-10 minutes or until the crust is golden brown and the cheese has melted.

9. Remove the pizza from the grill and let it cool for a few minutes.

10. Garnish with fresh basil leaves.

11. Drizzle balsamic glaze over the pizza.

12. Slice and serve hot.

Nutrition Information (per serving):

- Calories: 260

- Fat: 10g

- Carbohydrates: 30g

- Protein: 14g

Cooking Tips:

- To enhance the flavors, brush the rolled-out pizza dough with a little olive oil and sprinkle with garlic powder before adding the toppings.

- Use ripe and flavorful cherry tomatoes for the best taste.

- Drizzle the balsamic glaze lightly over the pizza or serve it on the side for dipping.

BBQ Chicken Flatbread

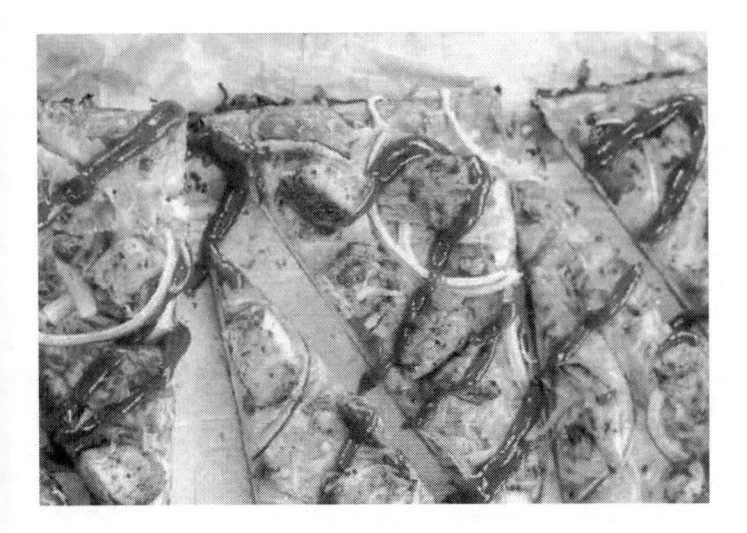

Grill Time: Approximately 15-20 minutes

Serving Size: 2-4 people

Ingredients:

- Flatbread or naan bread
- ¼ cup barbecue sauce
- 1 cup cooked chicken breast, shredded
- ¼ cup red onion, thinly sliced
- ¼ cup corn kernels
- 1 cup shredded mozzarella cheese
- Fresh cilantro leaves for garnish
- Salt and pepper to taste

Instructions:

1. Preheat your Ninja Woodfire Outdoor Grill and Smoker to medium-high heat.
2. Spread barbecue sauce evenly on the flatbread.
3. Arrange the shredded chicken, red onion, and corn kernels on top of the sauce.
4. Sprinkle the shredded mozzarella cheese over the toppings.
5. Season with salt and pepper to taste.
6. Carefully transfer the flatbread onto the grill grates.
7. Close the lid and cook for 5-8 minutes or until the cheese has melted and the edges are crispy.

8. Remove the flatbread from the grill and let it cool for a minute.

9. Garnish with fresh cilantro leaves.

10. Slice and serve warm.

Nutrition Information (per serving):

- Calories: 290

- Fat: 9g

- Carbohydrates: 30g

- Protein: 20g

Cooking Tips:

- For extra smoky flavor, grill the chicken breasts before shredding them.

- If you like a bit of heat, add sliced jalapenos or a drizzle of hot sauce to the flatbread before grilling.

- Serve with a side of ranch dressing or barbecue sauce for dipping.

Margherita Pizza with Grilled Peaches

Grill Time: Approximately 15-20 minutes

Serving Size: 2-4 people

Ingredients:

- Pizza dough (store-bought or homemade)

- ¼ cup pizza sauce

- 8 ounces fresh mozzarella cheese, sliced

- 2 ripe peaches, pitted and sliced

- Fresh basil leaves

- Balsamic glaze for drizzling
- Salt and pepper to taste

Instructions:

1. Preheat your Ninja Woodfire Outdoor Grill and Smoker to medium-high heat.
2. Roll out the pizza dough on a floured surface to your desired thickness.
3. Place the rolled-out dough on a pizza peel or a floured baking sheet.
4. Spread pizza sauce evenly over the dough, leaving a small border around the edges.
5. Arrange the mozzarella slices and sliced peaches on top of the sauce.
6. Season with salt and pepper to taste.
7. Carefully transfer the pizza from the peel or baking sheet onto the preheated grill grates.
8. Close the lid and cook for 8-10 minutes or until the crust is golden brown and the cheese has melted.
9. Remove the pizza from the grill and let it cool for a few minutes.
10. Garnish with fresh basil leaves.
11. Drizzle balsamic glaze over the pizza.
12. Slice and serve hot.

Nutrition Information (per serving):

- Calories: 280
- Carbohydrates: 35g
- Fat: 10g
- Protein: 14g

Cooking Tips:

- Grilling the peaches before adding them to the pizza enhances their natural sweetness and adds a smoky flavor.
- Use fresh and fragrant basil leaves for the best taste.
- Drizzle the balsamic glaze lightly over the pizza or serve it on the side for dipping.

Smoky Sausage & Mushroom Pizza

Grill Time: Approximately 15-20 minutes

Serving Size: 2-4 people

Ingredients:

- Pizza dough (store-bought or homemade)
- ¼ cup tomato sauce
- 8 ounces smoked sausage, sliced
- 1 cup mushrooms, sliced
- 1 cup shredded mozzarella cheese
- Fresh parsley leaves for garnish
- Salt and pepper to taste

Instructions:

1. Preheat your Ninja Woodfire Outdoor Grill and Smoker to medium-high heat.

2. Roll out the pizza dough on a floured surface to your desired thickness.

3. Place the rolled-out dough on a pizza peel or a floured baking sheet.

4. Spread tomato sauce evenly over the dough, leaving a small border around the edges.

5. Arrange the sliced smoked sausage and mushrooms on top of the sauce.

6. Sprinkle the shredded mozzarella cheese over the toppings.

7. Season with salt and pepper to taste.

8. Carefully transfer the pizza from the peel or baking sheet onto the preheated grill grates.

9. Close the lid and cook for 8-10 minutes or until the crust is golden brown and the cheese has melted.

10. Remove the pizza from the grill and let it cool.

Chapter 8

Yummy Smoker Burger & Sandwich Recipes

Smoky Bacon Cheddar Burger

Grill Time: Approximately 15-20 minutes

Serving Size: 4 burgers

Ingredients:

- 1.5 pounds ground beef
- ¼ cup barbecue sauce
- 4 slices cheddar cheese
- 8 slices bacon, cooked

- 4 hamburger buns
- Lettuce, tomato, and onion slices for topping
- Salt and pepper to taste

Instructions:

1. Preheat your Ninja Woodfire Outdoor Grill and Smoker to medium-high heat.
2. In a bowl, season the ground beef with salt and pepper, and mix well.
3. Divide the beef into 4 equal portions and shape them into patties.
4. Grill the patties on the preheated grill for 4-6 minutes per side, or until they reach the desired level of doneness.
5. During the last few minutes of grilling, brush each patty with barbecue sauce and place a slice of cheddar cheese on top.
6. Toast the hamburger buns on the grill for a minute or two.
7. Assemble the burgers by placing a patty on each bun, then layering with bacon, lettuce, tomato, and onion.
8. Serve hot.

Nutrition Information (per serving):

- Calories: 540
- Fat: 28g
- Carbohydrates: 32g
- Protein: 39g

Cooking Tips:

- For extra smoky flavor, use smoked cheddar cheese.
- If you prefer crispy bacon, you can cook it directly on the grill grates.
- Customize your toppings by adding pickles, avocado, or your favorite condiments.

Grilled Portobello Mushroom Burger

Grill Time: Approximately 15-20 minutes

Serving Size: 4 burgers

Ingredients:

- 4 large Portobello mushroom caps
- ¼ cup balsamic vinegar
- 2 tbsp. olive oil
- 4 hamburger buns
- 4 slices provolone cheese
- Arugula or spinach leaves for topping
- Salt and pepper to taste

Instructions:

1. Preheat your Ninja Woodfire Outdoor Grill and Smoker to medium-high heat.
2. In a small bowl, whisk together balsamic vinegar and olive oil.
3. Brush the mushroom caps with the vinegar-oil mixture on both sides.
4. Season the mushrooms with salt and pepper.
5. Place the mushroom caps on the grill grates and cook for 4-6 minutes per side, or until tender.
6. During the last few minutes of grilling, place a slice of provolone cheese on each mushroom cap.
7. Toast the hamburger buns on the grill for a minute or two.
8. Assemble the burgers by placing a mushroom cap on each bun, then topping with arugula or spinach.
9. Serve hot.

Nutrition Information (per serving):

- Calories: 240

- Fat: 12g

- Carbohydrates: 25g

- Protein: 12g

Cooking Tips:

- Marinate the mushroom caps for a more intense flavor. You can add garlic, herbs, or your preferred seasonings to the balsamic vinegar and olive oil mixture.

- For an extra kick, spread some pesto or spicy aioli on the buns before assembling the burgers.

- Add sliced tomatoes, red onions, or roasted bell peppers for extra freshness.

BBQ Pulled Pork Sandwich

Grill Time: Approximately 4-6 hours

Serving Size: 4 sandwiches

Ingredients:

- 2 pounds pork shoulder or butt

- 1 cup barbecue sauce
- ¼ cup apple cider vinegar
- 2 tbsp. brown sugar
- 1 tbsp. paprika
- 1 tbsp. garlic powder
- 1 tbsp. onion powder
- 1 tsp. salt
- ½ tsp. black pepper
- 4 hamburger buns
- Coleslaw for topping

Instructions:

1. Preheat your Ninja Woodfire Outdoor Grill and Smoker to 225°F (107°C) using indirect heat.
2. In a small bowl, mix together the brown sugar, paprika, garlic powder, onion powder, salt, and black pepper to make a dry rub.
3. Rub the dry rub mixture all over the pork shoulder.
4. Place the pork shoulder on the grill grates, close the lid, and smoke for 4-6 hours, or until the internal temperature reaches 195°F (90°C) and the meat is tender and easily shredded.
5. In a separate bowl, mix together the barbecue sauce and apple cider vinegar.
6. Remove the pork shoulder from the grill and let it rest for a few minutes. Then shred the meat using two forks.
7. Place the shredded pork in a large bowl and pour the barbecue sauce mixture over it. Mix until the meat is evenly coated.
8. Toast the hamburger buns on the grill for a minute or two.
9. Assemble the sandwiches by placing a generous amount of pulled pork on each bun and topping with coleslaw. Serve hot.

Nutrition Information (per serving):

- Calories: 550

- Fat: 20g

- Carbohydrates: 54g

- Protein: 36g

Cooking Tips:

- For the best flavor, use a bone-in pork shoulder or butt.

- Let the pork shoulder rest after smoking to allow the juices to redistribute and enhance the tenderness.

- If you prefer a spicier sandwich, add some hot sauce or red pepper flakes to the barbecue sauce mixture.

Grilled Chicken Caprese Sandwich

Grill Time: Approximately 15-20 minutes

Serving Size: 4 sandwiches

Ingredients:

- 4 boneless, skinless chicken breasts
- 4 tbsp. balsamic glaze
- 4 slices mozzarella cheese
- 4 slices tomato
- Fresh basil leaves
- 4 ciabatta rolls
- Salt and pepper to taste

Instructions:

1. Preheat your Ninja Woodfire Outdoor Grill and Smoker to medium-high heat.
2. Season the chicken breasts with salt and pepper.
3. Grill the chicken breasts on the preheated grill for 6-8 minutes per side, or until cooked through with no pink in the center.
4. During the last few minutes of grilling, brush each chicken breast with balsamic glaze and place a slice of mozzarella cheese on top.
5. Toast the ciabatta rolls on the grill for a minute or two.
6. Assemble the sandwiches by placing a chicken breast on each roll, then layering with tomato slices and fresh basil leaves.
7. Drizzle additional balsamic glaze on top if desired.
8. Serve hot.

Nutrition Information (per serving):

- Calories: 380
- Fat: 7g
- Carbohydrates: 36g
- Protein: 42g

Cooking Tips:

- Pound the chicken breasts to an even thickness before grilling to ensure even cooking.

- If you don't have balsamic glaze, you can make a quick version by simmering balsamic vinegar with a bit of honey or brown sugar until it thickens.

- For added flavor, brush the ciabatta rolls with garlic butter before toasting them on the grill.

Spicy Black Bean Burger

Grill Time: Approximately 15-20 minutes

Serving Size: 4 burgers

Ingredients:

- 1 can (15 ounces) black beans, drained and rinsed
- ½ cup bread crumbs
- ¼ cup chopped red bell pepper
- ¼ cup chopped onion
- 2 cloves garlic, minced
- 1 egg, beaten
- 1 tsp. chili powder
- ½ tsp. cumin
- ½ tsp. paprika
- Salt and pepper to taste
- 4 hamburger buns
- Avocado slices, lettuce, and tomato for topping

Instructions:

1. Preheat your Ninja Woodfire Outdoor Grill and Smoker to medium-high heat.
2. In a large bowl, mash the black beans with a fork or potato masher until they are mostly mashed but still have some texture.
3. Add the bread crumbs, red bell pepper, onion, garlic, beaten egg, chili powder, cumin, paprika, salt, and pepper to the bowl. Mix until well combined.
4. Shape the black bean mixture into 4 patties.
5. Grill the patties on the preheated grill for 4-6 minutes per side, or until heated through and slightly crispy on the outside.

6. Toast the hamburger buns on the grill for a minute or two.
7. Assemble the burgers by placing a black bean patty on each bun, then topping with avocado slices, lettuce, and tomato.
8. Serve hot.

Nutrition Information (per serving):

- Calories: 320

- Fat: 6g

- Carbohydrates: 53g

- Protein: 15g

Cooking Tips:

- If the black bean mixture is too wet to hold its shape, add a bit more bread crumbs until it reaches a better consistency.

- For extra heat, add chopped jalapeños or a dash of hot sauce to the black bean mixture.

- To prevent the patties from sticking to the grill, brush them with a bit of oil before grilling.

Teriyaki Pineapple Chicken Sandwich

Grill Time: Approximately 15-20 minutes

Serving Size: 4 sandwiches

Ingredients:

- 4 boneless, skinless chicken breasts
- ½ cup teriyaki sauce
- 4 pineapple slices

- 4 hamburger buns
- Lettuce and red onion slices for topping

Instructions

1. Preheat your Ninja Woodfire Outdoor Grill and Smoker to medium-high heat.
2. Place the chicken breasts in a resealable plastic bag and pour the teriyaki sauce over them. Seal the bag and marinate in the refrigerator for at least 30 minutes.
3. Remove the chicken breasts from the marinade and discard the excess marinade.
4. Grill the chicken breasts on the preheated grill for 6-8 minutes per side, or until cooked through with no pink in the center.
5. During the last few minutes of grilling, place a pineapple slice on top of each chicken breast.
6. Toast the hamburger buns on the grill for a minute or two.
7. Assemble the sandwiches by placing a chicken breast with pineapple on each bun, then topping with lettuce and red onion slices.
8. Serve hot.

Nutrition Information (per serving):

- Calories: 390

- Fat: 5g

- Carbohydrates: 47g

- Protein: 40g

Cooking Tips:

- If you prefer a stronger teriyaki flavor, baste the chicken breasts with additional teriyaki sauce while grilling.

- For added sweetness and caramelization, you can brush the pineapple slices with a little honey or brown sugar before placing them on the chicken.

- Serve the sandwich with a side of Asian slaw for a complete meal.

BBQ Brisket Sandwich

Grill Time: Approximately 8-10 hours

Serving Size: 4 sandwiches

Ingredients:

- 2 pounds beef brisket
- 1 cup barbecue sauce
- ¼ cup beef broth
- 2 tbsp. brown sugar
- 1 tbsp. smoked paprika
- 1 tbsp. garlic powder
- 1 tbsp. onion powder
- 1 tsp. salt
- ½ tsp. black pepper
- 4 hamburger buns
- Pickles and coleslaw for topping

Instructions:

1. Preheat your Ninja Woodfire Outdoor Grill and Smoker to 225°F (107°C) using indirect heat.
2. In a small bowl, mix together the brown sugar, smoked paprika, garlic powder, onion powder, salt, and black pepper to make a dry rub.
3. Rub the dry rub mixture all over the beef brisket, covering it evenly.
4. Place the beef brisket on the grill grates, close the lid, and smoke for 8-10 hours, or until the internal temperature reaches 200°F (93°C) and the meat is tender and easily shredded.

5. In a separate bowl, mix together the barbecue sauce and beef broth.

6. Remove the beef brisket from the grill and let it rest for a few minutes. Then shred the meat using two forks.

7. Place the shredded beef brisket in a large bowl and pour the barbecue sauce mixture over it. Mix until the meat is evenly coated.

8. Toast the hamburger buns on the grill for a minute or two.

9. Assemble the sandwiches by placing a generous amount of shredded brisket on each bun and topping with pickles and coleslaw.

10. Serve hot.

Nutrition Information (per serving):

- Calories: 570

- Fat: 22g

- Carbohydrates: 56g

- Protein: 37g

Cooking Tips:

- For the best texture and tenderness, choose a fatty cut of brisket.

- Wrap the brisket in aluminum foil halfway through the cooking process to help retain moisture.

- Serve the sandwich with a side of barbecue beans or corn on the cob for a classic barbecue feast.

Grilled Veggie Panini

Grill Time: Approximately 15-20 minutes

Serving Size: 4 sandwiches

Ingredients:

- 1 zucchini, sliced lengthwise

- 1 yellow squash, sliced lengthwise

- 1 red bell pepper, seeded and quartered

- 1 red onion, sliced into rounds

- ¼ cup balsamic vinegar

- 2 tbsp. olive oil

- 4 slices provolone cheese

- 4 ciabatta rolls

- Pesto or sun-dried tomato spread

- Salt and pepper to taste

Instructions:

1. Preheat your Ninja Woodfire Outdoor Grill and Smoker to medium-high heat.

2. In a small bowl, whisk together balsamic vinegar and olive oil.

3. Brush the zucchini, yellow squash, red bell pepper, and red onion slices with the balsamic-oil mixture on both sides.

4. Season the vegetables with salt and pepper.

5. Place the vegetables on the grill grates and cook for 3-4 minutes per side, or until they are tender and have grill marks.

6. During the last few minutes of grilling, place a slice of provolone cheese on each vegetable slice to melt slightly.

7. Slice the ciabatta rolls in half lengthwise and spread pesto or sun-dried tomato spread on one side of each roll.

8. Place the grilled vegetables on the bottom half of each roll, then top with the melted cheese.

9. Close the sandwiches with the top halves of the rolls.

10. Place the sandwiches on the grill and cook for 2-3 minutes per side, or until the bread is toasted and the cheese is fully melted.

11. Remove the sandwiches from the grill, let them cool slightly, and then slice them in half.

12. Serve hot.

Nutrition Information (per serving):

- Calories: 380

- Fat: 16g

- Carbohydrates: 46g

- Protein: 12g

Cooking Tips:

- Feel free to customize the vegetables based on your preferences. Eggplant, mushrooms, or asparagus would also work well in this recipe.

- You can use any type of bread or rolls for the Panini, such as sourdough or whole wheat.

- Add some fresh basil leaves or arugula to the sandwiches for an extra burst of flavor.

Caprese Grilled Cheese Sandwich

Grill Time: Approximately 10 minutes

Serving Size: 2 sandwiches

Ingredients:

- 4 slices sourdough bread
- 4 ounces fresh mozzarella cheese, sliced
- 2 medium tomatoes, sliced
- ¼ cup fresh basil leaves
- 2 tbsp. balsamic glaze
- 2 tbsp. butter, softened
- Salt and pepper to taste

Instructions:

1. Preheat a skillet or griddle over medium heat.
2. Butter one side of each slice of sourdough bread.
3. Place two slices of bread, buttered side down, on the skillet or griddle.
4. Layer the mozzarella cheese, tomato slices, and fresh basil leaves on each slice of bread.
5. Drizzle the balsamic glaze over the filling and sprinkle with salt and pepper.
6. Top each sandwich with the remaining slices of bread, buttered side up.
7. Cook the sandwiches for about 3-4 minutes per side, or until the bread is golden brown and the cheese is melted.
8. Remove the sandwiches from the skillet or griddle and let them cool slightly before slicing.
9. Serve warm.

Nutrition Information (per serving):

- Calories: 410

- Fat: 20g

- Carbohydrates: 42g

- Protein: 17g

Cooking Tips:

- If you don't have balsamic glaze, you can use a drizzle of balsamic vinegar instead.

- You can add a touch of garlic powder or dried Italian seasoning to enhance the flavors.

- Serve the sandwich with a side of mixed greens or a bowl of tomato soup for a complete meal.

Turkey Avocado Club Sandwich

Grill Time: Approximately 15 minutes

Serving Size: 2 sandwiches

Ingredients:

1. 6 slices whole wheat bread
2. 6 ounces sliced turkey breast
3. 4 slices cooked bacon
4. 1 ripe avocado, sliced
5. 2 lettuce leaves
6. 2 tomato slices
7. 2 tbsp. mayonnaise
8. Salt and pepper to taste

Instructions:

1. Toast the slices of bread until they reach your desired level of crispness.
2. Spread mayonnaise on one side of each slice of bread.
3. On two slices of bread, layer the turkey slices, bacon, avocado, lettuce, and tomato.
4. Sprinkle with salt and pepper.
5. Top each sandwich with the remaining slices of bread, mayonnaise side down.
6. Press the sandwiches together gently.
7. Slice each sandwich in half diagonally.
8. Serve immediately.

Nutrition Information (per serving):

- Calories: 470
- Fat: 25g
- Carbohydrates: 36g
- Protein: 27g

Cooking Tips:

- Feel free to add other toppings such as sliced red onion or cheese.
- For a healthier version, you can use turkey bacon or opt for low-fat mayonnaise.
- Serve the sandwich with a side of sweet potato fries or a fresh fruit salad.

Greek Gyro Wrap

Grill Time: Approximately 20 minutes

Serving Size: 4 wraps

Ingredients:

- 1 pound lamb or chicken, thinly sliced
- ¼ cup olive oil
- 2 tbsp. lemon juice
- 2 garlic cloves, minced
- 1 tsp. dried oregano
- Salt and pepper to taste
- 4 pita bread or flatbread wraps
- Tzatziki sauce (store-bought or homemade)
- Sliced cucumbers, tomatoes, and red onions
- Crumbled feta cheese
- Fresh parsley, chopped

Instructions:

1. In a bowl, whisk together the olive oil, lemon juice, minced garlic, dried oregano, salt, and pepper to make a marinade.

2. Add the sliced lamb or chicken to the marinade and toss to coat. Let it marinate for at least 15 minutes.

3. Preheat a skillet or grill pan over medium-high heat.

4. Cook the marinated meat for 3-4 minutes per side, or until cooked through.

5. Warm the pita bread or flatbread wraps according to the package instructions.

6. Spread a generous amount of tzatziki sauce on each wrap.

7. Place a few slices of cooked meat on each wrap, followed by sliced cucumbers, tomatoes, red onions, crumbled feta cheese, and chopped parsley.

8. Fold the sides of the wrap and roll it tightly.

9. Cut each wrap in half diagonally.

10. Serve warm.

Nutrition Information (per serving):

- Calories: 520

- Fat: 30g

- Carbohydrates: 35g

- Protein: 30g

Cooking Tips:

- You can add other traditional gyro fillings such as Kalamata olives or sliced bell peppers.

- If you prefer a vegetarian option, you can substitute the meat with grilled halloumi cheese or falafel.

- Serve the wraps with a side of Greek salad or roasted potatoes for a complete Greek-inspired meal.

Chapter 9

Flavorful Grilled Beef, Pork, & Chicken

Grilled Beef Burgers

Grill Time: Approximately 10-15 minutes

Serving Size: 4 burgers

Ingredients:

- 1 pound ground beef
- ¼ cup breadcrumbs
- 1 egg
- ¼ cup chopped onions
- 1 garlic clove, minced
- 1 tsp. Worcestershire sauce
- Salt and pepper to taste

Instructions:

1. Preheat the grill to medium heat.
2. In a bowl, combine ground beef, breadcrumbs, egg, chopped onions, minced garlic, Worcestershire sauce, salt, and pepper.
3. Mix the ingredients until well combined, then shape the mixture into 4 burger patties.

4. Place the burger patties on the preheated grill and cook for about 4-6 minutes per side or until cooked to your desired level of doneness.

5. Remove the burgers from the grill and let them rest for a few minutes before serving.

6. Serve on buns with your favorite toppings.

Nutrition Information (per serving):

- Calories: 300

- Fat: 15g

- Carbohydrates: 10g

- Protein: 30g

Cooking Tips:

- Use lean ground beef for healthier burgers.

- Create a small indentation in the center of each patty to prevent it from puffing up during cooking.

Grilled Pork Chops with Maple Glaze

Grill Time: Approximately 12-15 minutes

Serving Size: 4 pork chops

Ingredients:

- 4 bone-in pork chops (1 inch thick)
- ¼ cup maple syrup
- 2 tbsp. soy sauce
- 1 tbsp. Dijon mustard
- 2 garlic cloves, minced
- Salt and pepper to taste

Instructions:

1. Preheat the grill to medium-high heat.
2. In a small bowl, whisk together maple syrup, soy sauce, Dijon mustard, minced garlic, salt, and pepper to make the glaze.
3. Season the pork chops with salt and pepper.
4. Place the pork chops on the preheated grill and cook for about 6-8 minutes per side or until the internal temperature reaches 145°F (63°C).
5. Brush the glaze onto both sides of the pork chops during the last few minutes of cooking, allowing it to caramelize.
6. Remove the pork chops from the grill and let them rest for a few minutes before serving.
7. Serve hot.

Nutrition Information (per serving):

- Calories: 300

- Fat: 10g

- Carbohydrates: 16g

- Protein: 30g

Cooking Tips:

- For a smoky flavor, you can add wood chips to the grill.
- Use a meat thermometer to ensure the pork chops are cooked to the appropriate temperature.

Grilled Chicken Skewers with Lemon Herb Marinade

Grill Time: Approximately 15-20 minutes

Serving Size: 4 skewers

Ingredients:

- 1 pound boneless, skinless chicken breasts, cut into 1-inch cubes
- ¼ cup olive oil
- Juice of 1 lemon
- 2 garlic cloves, minced
- 1 tbsp. chopped fresh parsley
- 1 tbsp. chopped fresh basil
- Salt and pepper to taste

Instructions:

1. Preheat the grill to medium-high heat.
2. In a bowl, combine olive oil, lemon juice, minced garlic, chopped fresh parsley, chopped fresh basil, salt, and pepper to make the marinade.
3. Thread the chicken cubes onto skewers.
4. Place the chicken skewers on the preheated grill and cook for about 6-8 minutes, turning occasionally, or until the chicken is cooked through with no pink in the center.
5. Remove the chicken skewers from the grill and let them rest for a few minutes before serving.

6. Serve hot.

Nutrition Information (per serving):

- Calories: 200

- Fat: 10g

- Carbohydrates: 2g

- Protein: 25g

Cooking Tips:

- Soak wooden skewers in water for about 20 minutes before threading the chicken to prevent them from burning on the grill.

- Marinate the chicken for at least 30 minutes or up to overnight for maximum flavor.

Grilled Beef Kabobs with Vegetables

Grill Time: Approximately 12-15 minutes

Serving Size: 4 skewers

Ingredients:

- 1 pound beef sirloin, cut into 1-inch cubes
- 1 red bell pepper, cut into 1-inch pieces
- 1 yellow bell pepper, cut into 1-inch pieces
- 1 red onion, cut into 1-inchpieces
- 8-10 cherry tomatoes
- 2 tbsp. olive oil
- 2 tbsp. balsamic vinegar
- 2 garlic cloves, minced
- 1 tsp. dried thyme
- Salt and pepper to taste

Instructions:

1. Preheat the grill to medium-high heat.
2. In a small bowl, whisk together olive oil, balsamic vinegar, minced garlic, dried thyme, salt, and pepper to make the marinade.
3. Thread the beef cubes, bell pepper pieces, red onion pieces, and cherry tomatoes onto skewers, alternating the ingredients.
4. Brush the marinade onto the beef and vegetables.
5. Place the skewers on the preheated grill and cook for about 3-4 minutes per side or until the beef is cooked to your desired level of doneness and the vegetables are tender.
6. Remove the skewers from the grill and let them rest for a few minutes before serving.
7. Serve hot.

Nutrition Information (per serving):

- Calories: 250

- Fat: 14g

- Carbohydrates: 10g

- Protein: 20g

Cooking Tips:

- If using wooden skewers, soak them in water for about 20 minutes before threading the ingredients to prevent them from burning on the grill.

- Cut the beef and vegetables into similar-sized pieces for even cooking.

Grilled Pork Tenderloin with Mustard Glaze

Grill Time: Approximately 20-25 minutes

Serving Size: 4 servings

Ingredients:

- 1 pound pork tenderloin
- 2 tbsp. Dijon mustard
- 2 tbsp. honey
- 1 tbsp. soy sauce
- 1 tsp. minced fresh thyme
- 1 tsp. minced fresh rosemary
- Salt and pepper to taste

Instructions:

1. Preheat the grill to medium-high heat.

2. In a small bowl, whisk together Dijon mustard, honey, soy sauce, minced fresh thyme, minced fresh rosemary, salt, and pepper to make the glaze.

3. Season the pork tenderloin with salt and pepper.

4. Place the pork tenderloin on the preheated grill and cook for about 10-12 minutes, turning occasionally, or until the internal temperature reaches 145°F (63°C).

5. Brush the glaze onto the pork tenderloin during the last few minutes of cooking, allowing it to caramelize.

6. Remove the pork tenderloin from the grill and let it rest for a few minutes before slicing.

7. Slice the pork tenderloin and serve hot.

Nutrition Information (per serving):

- Calories: 220

- Fat: 5g

- Carbohydrates: 12g

- Protein: 30g

Cooking Tips:

- Let the pork tenderloin rest at room temperature for about 30 minutes before grilling to ensure even cooking.

- Use a meat thermometer to check for desired doneness. The internal temperature should be 145°F (63°C) for medium-rare and 160°F (71°C) for medium.

Grilled Chicken Caesar Salad

Grill Time: Approximately 15-20 minutes

Serving Size: 4 servings

Ingredients:

- 2 boneless, skinless chicken breasts
- 4 cups chopped romaine lettuce
- ½ cup Caesar dressing
- ¼ cup grated Parmesan cheese
- ¼ cup croutons
- Salt and pepper to taste

Instructions:

1. Preheat the grill to medium-high heat.
2. Season the chicken breasts with salt and pepper.
3. Place the chicken breasts on the preheated grill and cook for about 6-8 minutes per side or until the internal temperature reaches 165°F (74°C).
4. Remove the chicken breasts from the grill and let them rest for a few minutes before slicing.
5. Slice the chicken breasts into thin strips.
6. In a large bowl, combine the chopped romaine lettuce, Caesar dressing, grated Parmesan cheese, and croutons. Toss to coat the lettuce evenly.
7. Divide the salad among 4 plates and top each with the sliced grilled chicken.
8. Serve immediately.

Nutrition Information (per serving):

- Calories: 300
- Fat: 15g
- Carbohydrates: 12g
- Protein: 30g

Cooking Tips:

- Pound the chicken breasts to an even thickness before grilling for more even cooking.
- Customize the salad by adding additional toppings such as cherry tomatoes, sliced cucumbers, or grilled onions.

Grilled Pork Ribs with BBQ Sauce

Grill Time: Approximately 2-3 hours

Serving Size: 4 servings

Ingredients:

- 2 racks of pork ribs
- 1 cup barbecue sauce
- 2 tbsp. brown sugar
- 1 tbsp. paprika
- 1 tbsp. garlic powder
- 1 tbsp. onion powder
- Salt and pepper to taste

Instructions:

1. Preheat the grill to medium-low heat.
2. In a small bowl, mix together brown sugar, paprika, garlic powder, onion powder, salt, and pepper to make the dry rub.
3. Rub the dry rub mixture all over the pork ribs, coating them evenly.
4. Place the ribs on the grill, bone side down, and cook for about 2-3 hours, or until the meat is tender and pulls away easily from the bones.
5. During the last 15 minutes of cooking, brush the ribs with barbecue sauce, allowing it to caramelize.
6. Remove the ribs from the grill and let them rest for a few minutes before serving.

7. Serve hot with additional barbecue sauce on the side.

Nutrition Information (per serving):

- Calories: 500

- Fat: 35g

- Carbohydrates: 25g

- Protein: 25g

Cooking Tips:

- For a smokier flavor, add wood chips to the grill.

- Indirect heat cooking is recommended for ribs to ensure they cook slowly and become tender.

Grilled Chicken Fajitas

Grill Time: Approximately 15-20 minutes

Serving Size: 4 servings

Ingredients:

- 1 pound boneless, skinless chicken breasts
- 2 bell peppers (any color), sliced
- 1 large onion, sliced
- 2 tbsp. olive oil

- 2 tbsp. lime juice
- 2 tsp. chili powder
- 1 tsp. cumin
- 1 tsp. garlic powder
- ½ tsp. paprika
- Salt and pepper to taste
- Flour tortillas

Optional toppings: sour cream, guacamole, salsa, shredded cheese

Instructions:

1. Preheat the grill to medium-high heat.
2. In a small bowl, whisk together olive oil, lime juice, chili powder, cumin, garlic powder, paprika, salt, and pepper to make the marinade.
3. Place the chicken breasts, bell peppers, and onion slices in a large resealable bag or container. Pour the marinade over the ingredients, ensuring they are well coated. Marinate for at least 30 minutes or up to overnight.
4. Remove the chicken breasts, bell peppers, and onion slices from the marinade, allowing any excess marinade to drip off.
5. Place the chicken breasts, bell peppers, and onion slices on the preheated grill. Cook for about 6-8 minutes per side or until the chicken is cooked through and the vegetables are tender.
6. Remove the chicken, bell peppers, and onions from the grill and let them rest for a few minutes before slicing the chicken into strips.
7. Heat the flour tortillas on the grill for a minute on each side.
8. Serve the grilled chicken, bell peppers, and onions in the warmed tortillas. Add your desired toppings.
9. Roll up the tortillas and serve hot.

Nutrition Information (per serving):

- Calories: 350

- Fat: 10g

- Carbohydrates: 30g

- Protein: 35g

Cooking Tips:

- Slice the chicken, bell peppers, and onions into similar-sized pieces for even cooking.

- If using wooden skewers, soak them in water for about 20 minutes before threading the ingredients to prevent them from burning on the grill.

Grilled Pork Tenderloin with Herb Rub

Grill Time: Approximately 20-25 minutes

Serving Size: 4 servings

Ingredients:

- 1 pound pork tenderloin
- 2 tbsp. olive oil
- 2 cloves garlic, minced
- 1 tbsp. fresh rosemary, chopped
- 1 tbsp. fresh thyme, chopped
- 1 tsp. dried oregano
- 1 tsp. salt
- ½ tsp. black pepper

Instructions:

1. Preheat the grill to medium-high heat.

2. In a small bowl, combine olive oil, minced garlic, rosemary, thyme, dried oregano, salt, and black pepper to make the herb rub.

3. Rub the herb mixture all over the pork tenderloin, coating it evenly.

4. Place the pork tenderloin on the preheated grill and cook for about 8-10 minutes per side, or until the internal temperature reaches 145°F (63°C).

5. Remove the pork tenderloin from the grill and let it rest for a few minutes before slicing.

6. Slice the pork tenderloin into medallions and serve hot.

Nutrition Information (per serving):

- Calories: 250

- Fat: 12g

- Carbohydrates: 2g

- Protein: 30g

Chapter 10

Delicious Grilled Vegetarian Delights

Grilled Vegetable Skewers

Grill Time: 10-12 minutes

Serving Size: 4 servings

Ingredients:

- 2 zucchinis, sliced into rounds
- 1 red bell pepper, cut into chunks
- 1 yellow bell pepper, cut into chunks
- 1 red onion, cut into chunks
- 8 cherry tomatoes
- 8 button mushrooms
- 2 tbsp. olive oil
- 2 cloves garlic, minced
- 1 tsp. dried oregano
- Salt and pepper, to taste

Instructions:

1. Preheat your Ninja woodfire outdoor grill and smoker to medium-high heat.
2. In a bowl, combine the olive oil, minced garlic, dried oregano, salt, and pepper.
3. Thread the vegetables onto skewers, alternating the different vegetables.
4. Brush the vegetable skewers with the olive oil mixture, coating them evenly.
5. Place the skewers on the preheated grill and cook for 5-6 minutes per side, or until the vegetables are tender and lightly charred.
6. Remove from the grill and serve hot.

Nutrition Information per Serving:

- Calories: 120

- Protein: 3g

- Fat: 7g

- Carbohydrates: 14g

- Fiber: 4g

Cooking Tips:

- Soak wooden skewers in water for about 30 minutes before threading the vegetables to prevent them from burning.

Grilled Portobello Mushroom Burgers

Grill Time: 10-12 minutes

Serving Size: 4 servings

Ingredients:

- 4 large Portobello mushroom caps

- 4 burger buns

- 4 slices of cheese (optional)

- 4 lettuce leaves

- 4 tomato slices

- 4 red onion slices

- 2 tbsp. balsamic vinegar

- 2 tbsp. olive oil

- 2 cloves garlic, minced

- 1 tsp. dried thyme

- Salt and pepper, to taste

Instructions:

1. Preheat your Ninja woodfire outdoor grill and smoker to medium-high heat.
2. In a small bowl, whisk together the balsamic vinegar, olive oil, minced garlic, dried thyme, salt, and pepper.
3. Remove the stems from the Portobello mushrooms and brush both sides of the caps with the balsamic mixture.
4. Place the mushroom caps on the preheated grill and cook for 4-5 minutes per side, or until they are tender and grill marks appear.
5. Optional: During the last minute of grilling, place a slice of cheese on each mushroom cap to melt.
6. Remove the mushroom caps from the grill and assemble the burgers with buns, lettuce, tomato slices, and red onion slices.
7. Serve hot.

Nutrition Information per Serving:

- Calories: 250
- Protein: 9g
- Fat: 10g
- Carbohydrates: 32g
- Fiber: 5g

Cooking Tips:

- Marinating the Portobello mushroom caps enhances their flavor. You can let them marinate in the balsamic mixture for 15-30 minutes before grilling.

- If you prefer a vegan option, skip the cheese or use a vegan cheese alternative.

Smoked Stuffed Bell Peppers

Grill Time: 40-45 minutes

Serving Size: 4 servings

Ingredients:

- 4 bell peppers (any color), tops cut off and seeds removed
- 1 cup cooked quinoa
- 1 cup black beans, rinsed and drained
- 1 cup corn kernels
- ½ cup diced tomatoes
- ½ cup shredded cheddar cheese (optional)
- 2 tbsp. chopped fresh cilantro
- 1 tbsp. olive oil
- 1 tsp. ground cumin
- ½ tsp. chili powder
- Salt and pepper, to taste

Instructions:

1. Preheat your Ninja woodfire outdoor grill and smoker to medium heat.
2. In a large bowl, combine the cooked quinoa, black beans, corn kernels, diced tomatoes, shredded cheddar cheese (if using), chopped cilantro, olive oil, ground cumin, chili powder, salt, and pepper.
3. Spoon the quinoa mixture into the bell peppers, pressing it down to fill them completely.
4. Place the stuffed bell peppers on the preheated grill and close the lid. Smoke them for 30-35 minutes, or until the peppers are tender and the filling is heated through.
5. Remove from the grill and let them cool for a few minutes before serving.

Nutrition Information per Serving:

- Calories: 280

- Protein: 12g

- Fat: 8g

- Carbohydrates: 44g

- Fiber: 10g

Cooking Tips:

- You can customize the stuffing by adding other vegetables or spices according to your taste.

- For a vegan option, skip the cheese or use a vegan cheese alternative.

Grilled Halloumi Skewers

Grill Time: 6-8 minutes

Serving Size: 4 servings

Ingredients:

- 8 ounces halloumi cheese, cut into cubes

- 1 zucchini, sliced into rounds

- 1 yellow squash, sliced into rounds

- 1 red onion, cut into chunks

- 1 tbsp. olive oil

- 1 tbsp. lemon juice

- 1 tsp. dried oregano

- Salt and pepper, to taste

Instructions:

1. Preheat your Ninja woodfire outdoor grill and smoker to medium-high heat.
2. In a bowl, whisk together the olive oil, lemon juice, dried oregano, salt, and pepper.
3. Thread the halloumi cheese cubes, zucchini rounds, yellow squash rounds, and red onion chunks onto skewers, alternating the different ingredients.
4. Brush the skewers with the olive oil mixture, coating them evenly.
5. Place the skewers on the preheated grill and cook for 3-4 minutes per side, or until the halloumi cheese is golden brown and the vegetables are tender.
6. Remove from the grill and serve hot.

Nutrition Information per Serving:

- Calories: 220

- Protein: 12g

- Fat: 16g

- Carbohydrates: 9g

- Fiber: 2g

Cooking Tips:

- Halloumi cheese holds its shape well on the grill, making it perfect for skewers.

- Soak wooden skewers in water for about 30 minutes before threading the ingredients to prevent them from burning.

Smoked Stuffed Portobello Mushrooms

Grill Time: 25-30 minutes

Serving Size: 4 servings

Ingredients:

- 4 large Portobello mushroom caps
- 1 cup cooked quinoa
- 1 cup baby spinach, chopped
- ½ cup crumbled feta cheese
- ¼ cup sun-dried tomatoes, chopped
- 2 cloves garlic, minced
- 2 tbsp. chopped fresh basil
- 1 tbsp. balsamic vinegar
- 1 tbsp. olive oil
- Salt and pepper, to taste

Instructions:

1. Preheat your Ninja woodfire outdoor grill and smoker to medium heat.
2. In a bowl, combine the cooked quinoa, chopped baby spinach, crumbled feta cheese, chopped sun-dried tomatoes, minced garlic, chopped fresh basil, balsamic vinegar, olive oil, salt, and pepper.
3. Remove the stems from the Portobello mushrooms and scrape out the gills with a spoon.
4. Spoon the quinoa mixture into the mushroom caps, pressing it down to fill them completely.

5. Place the stuffed Portobello mushrooms on the preheated grill and close the lid. Smoke them for 20-25 minutes, or until the mushrooms are tender and the filling is heated through.

6. Remove from the grill and let them cool for a few minutes before serving.

Nutrition Information per Serving:

- Calories: 220

- Protein: 10g

- Fat: 9g

- Carbohydrates: 27g

- Fiber: 5g

Cooking Tips:

- You can add additional ingredients to the stuffing, such as chopped olives or diced bell peppers, for extra flavor.

- For a vegan option, skip the feta cheese or use a vegan cheese alternative.

BBQ Tofu Skewers

Grill Time: 10-12 minutes

Serving Size: 4 servings

Ingredients:

- 1 block firm tofu, pressed and cut into cubes
- ½ cup barbecue sauce
- 2 tbsp. soy sauce
- 2 tbsp. maple syrup
- 1 tbsp. apple cider vinegar
- 1 tsp. smoked paprika
- 1 tsp. garlic powder
- Salt and pepper, to taste
- Wooden skewers, soaked in water

Instructions:

1. In a bowl, whisk together the barbecue sauce, soy sauce, maple syrup, apple cider vinegar, smoked paprika, garlic powder, salt, and pepper.
2. Thread the tofu cubes onto soaked wooden skewers.
3. Brush the tofu skewers with the barbecue sauce mixture, coating them evenly.
4. Preheat your Ninja woodfire outdoor grill and smoker to medium-high heat.
5. Place the skewers on the preheated grill and cook for 5-6 minutes per side, or until the tofu is lightly charred and heated through.
6. Remove from the grill and serve hot.

Nutrition Information per Serving:

- Calories: 180
- Protein: 12g
- Fat: 5g
- Carbohydrates: 25g
- Fiber: 2g

Cooking Tips:

- Pressing the tofu before marinating and grilling helps remove excess moisture and allows it to absorb more flavor.

- Soak wooden skewers in water for about 30 minutes before threading the tofu cubes to prevent them from burning.

Grilled Veggie Quesadillas

Grill Time: 10-12 minutes

Serving Size: 4 servings

Ingredients:

- 4 large flour tortillas
- 1 zucchini, sliced into strips
- 1 yellow squash, sliced into strips
- 1 red bell pepper, sliced into strips
- 1 red onion, sliced
- 1 cup shredded Monterey Jack cheese
- 1 tbsp. olive oil
- 1 tsp. ground cumin
- ½ tsp. chili powder
- Salt and pepper, to taste
- Salsa, guacamole, and sour cream (for serving)

Instructions:

1. Preheat your Ninja woodfire outdoor grill and smoker to medium-high heat.

2. In a bowl, toss the zucchini, yellow squash, red bell pepper, and red onion with olive oil, ground cumin, chili powder, salt, and pepper.

3. Place the vegetables on the preheated grill and cook for 4-5 minutes per side, or until they are tender and lightly charred.

4. Remove the grilled vegetables from the grill and set aside.

5. Lay a tortilla flat and sprinkle half of it with shredded Monterey Jack cheese. Top with grilled vegetables and fold the tortilla in half.

6. Repeat with the remaining tortillas and filling.

7. Place the quesadillas on the grill and cook for 2-3 minutes per side, or until the cheese is melted and the tortillas are crispy.

8. Remove from the grill, let them cool for a minute, then slice into wedges.

9. Serve hot with salsa, guacamole, and sour cream.

Nutrition Information per Serving:

- Calories: 320

- Protein: 12g

- Fat: 16g

- Carbohydrates: 35g

- Fiber: 4g

Cooking Tips:

- You can add other vegetables like corn kernels or mushrooms to the quesadillas for extra flavor and texture.

- If you prefer a spicier kick, add some chopped jalapenos or a sprinkle of cayenne pepper.

Smoked Stuffed Zucchini Boats

Grill Time: 30-35 minutes

Serving Size: 4 servings

Ingredients:

- 2 large zucchinis
- 1 cup cooked quinoa
- 1 cup marinara sauce
- 1 cup shredded mozzarella cheese
- ¼ cup grated Parmesan cheese
- 2 cloves garlic, minced
- 2 tbsp. chopped fresh basil
- 1 tbsp. olive oil
- Salt and pepper, to taste

Instructions:

1. Preheat your Ninja woodfire outdoor grill and smoker to medium heat.
2. Cut the zucchinis in half lengthwise and scoop out the center to create boats.
3. In a bowl, combine the cooked quinoa, marinara sauce, shredded mozzarella cheese, grated Parmesan cheese, minced garlic, chopped fresh basil, olive oil, salt, and pepper.

4. Spoon the quinoa mixture into the zucchini boats, pressing it down to fill them completely.

Conclusion

Congratulations on completing your culinary journey with the Ninja Woodfire Outdoor Grill! We hope this cookbook has inspired you to explore the world of grilling and experiment with delicious flavors and techniques.

Throughout this cookbook, we've shared a variety of appetizers, meats, seafood, vegetarian options, sides, sauces, marinades, rubs, and even desserts that you can prepare on your Ninja Woodfire Grill. We hope these recipes have allowed you to discover new flavors, techniques, and combinations that will impress your family and friends.

In addition to the recipes, we've provided essential information on getting started with the Ninja Woodfire Grill, including safety guidelines and tips for successful grilling. We believe that understanding the grill and following proper safety precautions are crucial for a great grilling experience.

Remember, grilling is not just about the food—it's an opportunity to gather with loved ones, create lasting memories, and savor the joy of outdoor cooking. The Ninja Woodfire Outdoor Grill offers a versatile and convenient way to bring that experience to your backyard.

As you continue your grilling adventures, don't be afraid to experiment, customize recipes to your taste, and explore new ingredients. The possibilities are endless, and the Ninja Woodfire Grill is your trusted companion in creating culinary masterpieces.

More also, we would like to remind you of the importance of proper grill maintenance and cleaning. Regular maintenance will not only extend the lifespan of your grill but also ensure optimal performance for future grilling sessions. Refer to the tips provided in this cookbook to keep your Ninja Woodfire Grill in excellent condition.

Acknowledgement

We would like to express our gratitude to all the contributors, chefs, and grilling enthusiasts who helped make this cookbook possible. Their expertise, creativity, and passion for grilling have enriched this collection of recipes.

Lastly, we hope this cookbook has ignited your passion for grilling and brought joy to your outdoor cooking experience. May your culinary adventures continue to be filled with delicious flavors, happy gatherings, and unforgettable moments around the grill.

Happy grilling!

[*Kaida Emberwood*]

Printed in Great Britain
by Amazon

024a5bf0-f6c5-45d3-aae5-b7a74d712498R01